AIDS

AIDS

A HANDBOOK
FOR THE FUTURE

Marianne LeVert

The Millbrook Press • Brookfield, Connecticut

JUN 0 2 1997

ABF 4150

Library of Congress Cataloging-in-Publication Data
LeVert, Marianne.
AIDS : a handbook for the future / Marianne LeVert.
p. cm.
Includes bibliographical references and index.
ISBN 1-56294-660-9 (lib. bdg.)
1. AIDS (Disease)—Juvenile literature.   I. Title.
RC607.A26L476 1996
616.97'92—dc20 96-3186 CIP

Photographs courtesy of UPI/Bettmann: pp. 13, 80, 114; Dr. M. A. Gonda,
NCI-Frederick Cancer Research and Development Center: p. 32 (top);
K. Nagashima, NCI-Frederick Cancer Research and Development Center:
p. 32 (bottom); CDC National AIDS Clearinghouse, U.S. Department of
Health and Human Services: pp. 40, 134; Wide World Photos: pp. 59, 87,
109, 121, 130. Diagram on p. 63 by Frank Senyk.

Published by The Millbrook Press, Inc.
Brookfield, Connecticut

Contents

AIDS

1

AIDS Today

Kathy was only twenty-three years old when she received a phone call that changed her life forever. She remembers that she was getting ready for a class and was hurrying to get to campus on time. Even though it had been several years, Kathy immediately recognized the voice on the other end of the line. It was Lenore, her ex-husband's mother. Barely able to speak, Lenore left a brief message: "John has AIDS. We thought you should know because you probably should be tested."

Kathy was in shock. She went to class that night, but she could not concentrate on the teacher's words and left early. As she drove home, she felt tears rolling down her cheeks. She was thinking of John and his family, who had been such important people in her life.

Kathy and John had met when they were eighteen years old and were married a year later. Although they cared deeply for each other and hoped to make a life together, their marriage simply did not work. John often seemed unhappy and withdrawn. Kathy always felt that he was holding something back from the relationship, maybe even hiding something from her. She suspected that he was seeing someone else during their marriage. After they separated, friends told her that he had been seeing other people—both women and men. To this day Kathy does not know if this is true, but she feels that it may explain why he was so unhappy. And it may explain how he became infected with HIV years before.

Kathy took Lenore's advice and did get tested. Unfortunately, the results showed that Kathy was also infected with HIV, the virus that causes AIDS. "The day I received the results of my HIV test was the worst day of my life. I did not want to die, but I was more scared of getting really sick. I have done everything possible to stay healthy," she says.

Six years later, energetic and enthusiastic as ever, Kathy is an HIV/AIDS educator and counselor. Hoping to prevent others from contracting this dangerous virus, she frequently shares her experiences with young people who are learning about AIDS in school. Still healthy after ten years, Kathy remains optimistic about her future. She recently celebrated her twenty-ninth birthday by buying a condominium. "I decided to take out a thirty-year mortgage," she says with a smile.

Kathy is one of almost a million Americans now infected with the human immunodeficiency virus, known as HIV. Infected at age nineteen, Kathy belongs to another group whose numbers are increasing at alarming rates: teenagers infected with HIV. Researchers estimate that more than 20 percent of all Americans with AIDS (acquired immune deficiency syndrome) were infected when they were in their teens. Worldwide, almost half of the people with AIDS were infected as teenagers.

A NEW AWARENESS

AIDS is very much on the minds of young people, parents, medical experts, educators, and the millions of Americans who are infected with or affected by HIV. AIDS has been the topic of countless books, news programs, school courses, and dinner-time conversations across the country. Many famous entertainers, sports figures, doctors, and public officials have generously and poignantly shared their experiences, raised money for research, made informational videos, and dedicated their time and money to increase public understanding of the disease. Some, like basketball star Magic Johnson, are living with HIV. Some, like MTV star Pedro Zamora, young activist Ryan White, and tennis star Arthur Ashe, have died from AIDS.

In addition to many well-known speakers and health activists, countless numbers of everyday people have joined the effort to prevent the spread of AIDS, raise money for research, and improve the quality of life for people living with AIDS. In cities, small towns, and rural communities throughout the country, dedicated volunteers help others by delivering meals to people with AIDS, visiting and caring for babies with AIDS in hospitals, sponsoring educational workshops, and operating information hotlines.

FEAR OF THE UNKNOWN

It has taken our society many years to reach this level of knowledge and compassion. When the first AIDS cases were reported in 1981, no one knew exactly what caused the disease or how others became infected. Understandably, many people were frightened and wanted to protect themselves and their families from being exposed to the virus. Some proposed separating or quarantining people with AIDS. In some communities, anger and suspicion gave rise to very hurtful actions against people with AIDS. Gay men and injection drug users, already treated as outcasts by much of our society, were among the first people with AIDS. They were often the targets of society's fear and anger.

Even when public-heath officials determined that AIDS was caused by a virus that was transmitted through the exchange of body fluids, specifically semen, vaginal secretions, and blood, and not through casual contact, many people continued to shun people with AIDS. Employers fired or refused to hire people who had AIDS or might be at risk of contracting it. Ambulance drivers refused to transport AIDS patients to hospitals. Police in several cities wore anti-AIDS masks. In many places, even young children were the targets of discrimination. In Florida, a few residents went so far as to burn down the house of a family whose children had AIDS.

RYAN WHITE

Ryan White was only twelve years old when he was infected with HIV. Ryan had hemophilia, a hereditary disease that causes severe blood-clotting defi-

Ryan White, shown here with classmates at age fifteen, was infected with AIDS at age twelve through a blood transfusion. Ryan spoke at schools, on national television programs, and before political leaders in the hope of educating people about the disease. He died in 1990 at age eighteen.

ciencies, and needed injections of a blood product called Factor VIII so his blood would clot properly. Like thousands of other hemophiliacs in the early 1980s, Ryan had been infected by HIV-contaminated blood.

When his medical condition became known to his community in Kokomo, Indiana, some teachers and parents feared he could infect other students. They asked that he not come to school. Other children and classmates teased him and avoided him on the street. Ryan was determined to attend school like every other child and to be treated with decency and respect. He took the matter to court and won the right to attend school in 1986. In the process, Ryan decided that the best way to change people's attitudes was to educate them. So Ryan went to schools and answered students' questions about AIDS, about sickness, and about death. Featured on national news programs, Ryan won the hearts of millions of people with his honesty, determination, and bravery. Until his death in 1990, he became a national figure in AIDS awareness.

AIDS

"A lot of people would back away from me on the street. They'd run from me. Maybe I would have been afraid of AIDS, too, but I wouldn't have been mean."

Ryan White
People Magazine
April 23, 1988

When Ryan died at age eighteen, more than a thousand people attended memorial services for him, including First Lady Barbara Bush and entertainer Michael Jackson. Singer Elton John, who had kept a week-long vigil with the White family in the hospital, sang and dedicated "Candle in the Wind" to Ryan at a Farm Aid concert the week Ryan died, a moving tribute to a life cut short. Ryan is credited with helping to change our society's attitude toward this disease and the people who have it. He also left another legacy: The Ryan White Comprehensive AIDS Resources Act, passed shortly after his death in 1990, provides funds to state and local AIDS education, care, and prevention programs.

COMBATING ISOLATION AND REJECTION

In great part due to the efforts of Ryan White and other AIDS activists, extreme incidents of discrimination and cruelty toward people with AIDS have decreased. There are, however, many people with AIDS who are not treated properly. Although the Americans with Disabilities Act protects people who are sick or disabled from being treated unfairly when they seek housing, medical attention, and employment, people with AIDS experience job, housing, insurance, and other kinds of discrimination today. And despite overwhelming scientific evidence that AIDS is not spread through casual contact, many people are so fearful about this virus that they shun friends and relatives.

"My cousin Richie has AIDS," explains Jean. "Of course, most people in the family don't see him anymore. They're just too

afraid. I know they say you can't catch it just by being in the same room, but I'm still not sure about that. I know I'd never let my kids go near him. I hear he was into drugs years ago, so he really brought this on himself."

Richie's relatives told him that he was not welcome at the family Christmas party. They did not want to risk "catching" AIDS from him.

Although a new spirit of understanding and goodwill is slowly replacing fear and anger, there are still far too many people like Richie—men and women with AIDS who suffer and die alone. To counter such isolation and rejection, a growing number of dedicated volunteers are working to make life better for people with AIDS.

Joan Rexford is one such volunteer. Her son Chris died of AIDS. During the last four years of his life, he was hospitalized at least seven times. When she visited her son each day, Joan met many AIDS patients who had no support at all—no visitors at the hospital and no one to care for them when they were released. After Chris died, she decided to change that situation. Today she visits people with AIDS in the hospital and provides supportive services to people with AIDS in the community. Her kindness and generosity are making an enormous difference in the lives of people with AIDS.

In addition to wonderful professional and volunteer people like Joan, there are numerous community organizations that provide social and medical services to people with AIDS and people at risk of contracting

HIV. Due largely to an increase in educational programs in schools and publicity in the media, Americans are aware that this deadly virus is present in communities throughout the United States and the world. Most also are aware that anyone who engages in unprotected sex or shares needles or syringes is at risk for contracting HIV, including both men and women; homosexuals and heterosexuals; and adults, young adults, and teens.

A GROWING THREAT

Tragically, despite heightened public awareness, the virus continues to spread throughout the United States—especially among women, teens, and young adults. There are people with HIV infection and AIDS in every state in the country, every age group, economic bracket, of both sexes and all sexual orientations. Of particular concern to the medical community, to families, and to educators is the rapid rate of infection among teens and young adults: At least 20 percent of people with AIDS in the United States were infected in their teens. Although still a small percentage of total AIDS cases in the United States, the number of teenagers with AIDS is doubling every year, making AIDS the sixth-leading cause of death among teens.

AIDS

Ninety percent of HIV-infected people live in developing countries.

Experts estimate that nearly one million Americans are now infected with HIV, including perhaps as many as 200,000 teens and young adults. Because it can take as long as ten years for symptoms to appear after HIV infection, most infected people do not even know they are carrying the virus. If they are sexually active, they can pass HIV to their partners, who can pass it to others, who can pass it to others, and so on. This is one way the AIDS epidemic continues to spread.

In 1994, AIDS became the leading cause of death among Americans aged twenty-five to forty-four. These are often the most productive years in our lives—the time when we fall in love, start families, and embark upon careers or work to support our families. The loss of so many young people to disabling illness and early death is a global tragedy.

Of course, for every person infected with HIV, there are dozens of others whose lives are changed forever. Spouses, lovers, children, parents, teachers, friends, and neighbors are all profoundly affected. Throughout the world, millions of children already have lost a parent, usually the mother, to AIDS. Officials estimate that by the year 2000, there will be about 125,000 of these children in the United States, including at least 30,000 children in New York City alone. In Africa, where the epidemic is far worse than in this country, experts estimate that nearly 10 million children will be orphaned by AIDS by the beginning of the twenty-first century.[1] In poor countries and communities in the United States, the children left behind are more vulnerable to neglect, malnutrition, and disease.

AIDS is now a pandemic—a disease that exists in every country in the world. To date, about 4.5 million people in the world have been diagnosed with AIDS. Experts estimate that 18 million adults and 1.5 million children are infected with HIV. Each year these numbers increase by millions. Experts predict that by the year 2000, at least 30 to 40 million people will be infected with the virus.

Africa, where most researchers believe the virus began at least several decades ago, has been the hardest hit by the AIDS epidemic. Ten million people living in countries located below the Sahara Desert are believed to be infected with HIV—accounting for about 60 pecent of all the HIV infections in the world. In Rwanda, Uganda, Burundi, Zaire, Mozambique, and Zimbabwe, widespread poverty, poor health and nutrition, famine, and civil strife are speeding the spread of the virus.

Health officials are equally concerned about the spread of HIV in Asia, which is increasing so fast that the epidemic there may well surpass that of Africa by the year 2000. By 1996, about 2.5 million people in Asia were infected with the virus—an increase of a million in only a year's time. The epidemic is exploding especially in Thailand, Cambodia, Vietnam, and India. Latin American and Caribbean countries are also at risk for huge increases in HIV infections and AIDS cases. "We are only at the beginning of the HIV epidemic in the world," warns Dr. James Curran, former associate director for HIV/AIDS at the Centers for Disease Control and Prevention (CDC).[2] International health officials hope that world leaders will take immediate action to curb the spread of AIDS in their countries by educating and protecting their citizens.

A GROWING BODY OF KNOWLEDGE

The AIDS epidemic is now in its second decade. Although there is no cure or preventive vaccine yet, medical experts have learned a tremendous amount about this deadly, but preventable, disease:

- AIDS is caused by a virus that slowly destroys the body's ability to fight infection and disease.
- An average of eleven years transpires between HIV infection and the onset of AIDS.
- AIDS is spread through vaginal, oral, and anal sex, and contaminated needles, syringes, and blood products. It also can be passed to an unborn child through an infected mother's bloodstream or to her child through breast milk.
- AIDS is a devastating illness not only for those who are infected, but also for their communities, friends, and families.
- There are steps that people can take to reduce their risk of contracting the virus.

With attention to the unique concerns and questions of young adults, this book will explore the complex medical, social, and political issues that surround the spread, the treatment, and the prevention of AIDS.

We will hear the personal experiences of young men and women who are living with HIV infection and AIDS, families who have lost loved ones to AIDS, caregivers who support and improve the quality of life of people with AIDS, and community educators who are helping to save the lives of others.

2

The AIDS Virus and the Immune System

HIV. AIDS. In less than two decades, these acronyms have become virtually household terms. Most teens and adults, and even many children, are aware that HIV is a very dangerous and contagious virus that causes AIDS. It may be hard for most of us to imagine a world without AIDS, but the virus that causes this disease is probably quite new. Many scientists believe that the virus may have originated in Africa in the late 1950s. It came to the attention of health officials in the United States very suddenly in the early 1980s.

THE DISCOVERY OF THE VIRUS

In early 1981, doctors in Los Angeles began seeing very serious and unusual infections among a handful of young men. In addition to swollen glands and severe weight loss, all of the men had pneumocystis carinii pneumonia (PCP), a dangerous and rare lung infection that usually strikes a person whose body is unable to fight infections. All the men lived near Los Angeles. All were homosexuals, aged thirty-five or younger. All died within months of being seen.

Alarmed, the doctors reported these cases to the Centers for Disease Control and Prevention (CDC), the federal agency in charge of investigating and monitoring diseases in the United States. Although researchers at the CDC suspected right away that the disease might be spread through sexual contact, no one knew the cause of this condition. No one even had a name for it. The CDC issued its first notice about these cases in June 1981 in its weekly report about diseases in the United States. It was read by physicians and other medical personnel throughout the country. Many of them had seen patients with similar symptoms during the previous several years.

Dr. James Curran, then head of the CDC's Venereal Disease division, immediately began receiving reports from New York, New Jersey, and California. By midsummer, fifteen more cases of PCP were reported to Dr. Curran and his colleagues, as well as yet another baffling condition: Kaposi's sarcoma (KS), an extremely rare form of skin cancer. Very quickly, the CDC received reports of hundreds of similar illnesses affecting gay men. In addition to PCP and Kaposi's sarcoma, these patients suffered from other symptoms and infections. The most common included swollen glands, fevers, extreme weight loss, a rare form of tuberculosis, and several viruses and infections not normally harmful to people. Public-health officials were concerned that a new, contagious disease was present in the country.

One of the most striking characteristics common to these patients was the damaged condition of their immune systems. Blood tests showed that all the patients lacked sufficient amounts of certain disease-fighting white blood cells called T-lymphocytes or T-cells. These important cells are the directors of the immune system, the body's complex and powerful system of defense against infection and illness. When the immune system is damaged, the body cannot fight disease. Medical experts use the term immunodeficiency to describe this condition. Because the earliest cases were believed to be only among gay men, the experts first called the disease Gay-Related Immunodeficiency Syndrome (GRID).

Within a year, however, doctors began seeing other groups of people with immunodeficiency and life-threatening infections, diseases, and cancers. Some were injection drug users, some were these drug users' sexual partners, some were women, and some were recipients of blood products and blood transfusions. By the end of 1981, about 265 cases were reported in the United States. Fifteen were children. In 1983 the first cases from Africa were reported—all heterosexual men and women. Clearly, this was not a disease that affected only gay men. And it was present in many countries of the world.

As this baffling disease spread throughout the world and as more men, women, and children became deathly ill, scientists on both sides of the Atlantic Ocean tried to find the source of this terrible sickness and death. Dr. Robert Gallo at the Institutes of Health in Bethesda, Maryland, headed up the American research team. Dr. Luc Montagnier at the Louis Pasteur Institute in Paris, France, directed studies in his country. Often these two institutes worked cooperatively, sharing important experiments and findings with each other. As the world turned its attention to their work, however, the scientists became increasingly competitive. Whoever found the answer to this mystery, they knew, would be certain to receive worldwide recognition.

After intensive experiments, researchers from both the United States and France announced in 1984 that they had isolated the cause of this deadly disease. After a long, bitter battle, the scientific community now credits Dr. Luc Montagnier with this important discovery. The culprit, he said, was a rare kind of virus called a retrovirus. The virus did its damage by infecting, multiplying within, and then destroying the body's T-cells.

HIV: HUMAN IMMUNODEFICIENCY VIRUS

After several name changes, public-health officials agreed to call this infectious agent HIV, which stands for human immunodeficiency virus. HIV infection, as researchers quickly discovered, can last for many years without any visible symptoms of illness. Doctors now suspect that during this seemingly "quiet" time, a tremendous battle takes place between the immune system and the virus. In fact, HIV may be multiplying at the rate of a billion viruses a day and invading healthy blood cells. Meanwhile, various immune system cells and chemicals respond immediately by multiplying and attacking the virus.

AIDS

"The first thing (the epidemic) brought was exile."

Albert Camus
The Plague

During the last stage of HIV infection, however, the immune system begins to lose the battle against the virus and can no longer defend the body against infections. All kinds of germs then take the "opportunity" to invade and infect the body. These infections are called opportunistic infections.

The final stage of HIV infection is called AIDS, acquired immune deficiency syndrome. People are said to have AIDS when they have very few T-cells left and/or they become sick with one or more opportunistic infections. After fighting these illnesses for several years, many people with AIDS die.

Within a year of the first cases, researchers knew how this virus is transmitted or passed from one person to another: HIV is transmitted through the exchange of certain body fluids, including semen, vaginal secretions, and blood. HIV is called a sexually transmitted disease (STD) because one of the ways it can be spread is through vaginal, anal, or oral sex. HIV also can be spread through the exchange of infected blood.

Injection drug users, for instance, can contract HIV if they use needles that contain HIV-infected blood. During the early 1980s, thousands of people became infected through blood transfusions and blood products. By 1985, researchers had developed a procedure to test blood for HIV infection and, as a result, our country's blood supply is now safe.

We also know that an infected woman can transmit the virus during pregnancy, childbirth, and breast-feeding. Although there is still a lot that we don't know about AIDS, we have learned much in a very short time about this unique virus.

MICROORGANISMS

A person who has AIDS is suffering from one or more specific opportunistic infections. Many of these infections are caused by common germs found in everyday life. If the immune system is working properly, these germs are not harmful to us. The world we live in is full of countless microorganisms or microbes, living things that are too small to be seen without a microscope. They are present on our skin, in our mouths, in the air we breathe, the soil we walk on, the water we drink and swim in, and the objects we touch. Most of these microbes coexist with us peacefully, and many actually are beneficial to humans, animals, plants, and soil. Some, called pathogens or, more commonly, germs, can cause infection and disease. The most common pathogens that can harm humans are protozoans, fungi, certain bacteria, and viruses.

Protozoans are parasites, microscopic one-celled animals that live off other organisms or cells, found in salt and fresh water, damp sand, soil, and moss. Some parasites move from these environments into the bodies of insects and animals, where they continue to grow and mature. The protozoans that cause malaria, for instance, mature inside an anopheles mosquito, and the protozoans that cause sleeping sickness live inside several species of tsetse fly. After entering a human's bloodstream, they feed off various parts of the body and often destroy them. The liver and red blood cells are first choices for malaria parasites; the heart and brain for sleeping-sickness parasites.

Fungi are simple plants that feed on living or dead organisms. Mushrooms, yeast, and molds are common fungi. Some fungi, like those used to make vitamins, medicines, bread, and cheese, are very useful to humans. Others cause infections like athlete's foot, thrush, and vaginal yeast infections. Usually treatable with medicine, fungal infections, although uncomfortable and irritating, are rarely dangerous.

Bacteria are one-celled life forms that do not depend on a host cell to survive. Because each bacterium cell contains a chromosome—the genetic material necessary for survival and reproduction—this organism is capable of living and reproducing practically anywhere. By duplicating its chromosome and then dividing in half, the bacterium is able to reproduce very rapidly. Although beneficial bacteria far outnumber those that cause disease, there are, nevertheless, numerous bacteria whose toxins or poisons are capable of harming—even destroying—vital tissues and cells in our body. Streptococcus, toxic-shock syndrome, and tuberculosis are examples of serious, contagious, and potentially fatal bacterial infections. Fortunately, most bacterial infections respond to antibiotic drugs.

Viruses are very tiny, very simple microorganisms. Made up essentially of a strand or strands of genetic material called deoxyribonucleic acid (DNA) wrapped in a coat of protein, a virus can't live or reproduce on its own. In order to grow and reproduce, viruses need living cells; without them, they are basically just bits of chemical matter. Once they have found suitable cells or hosts, they are able to reproduce and cause disease and infection.

Smaller than the blood cells in our body, viruses first attach themselves to cells and then slip inside where they release a substance called nucleoprotein.

This substance transmits the DNA of the virus to the DNA of the healthy cell. The virus, in effect, has "hijacked" the host cell's instructions for making copies of itself. Instead of reproducing itself, the host cell makes protein coats for new viruses. The host cell then becomes a virtual virus-producing factory. Eventually the host cell bursts open and dies, spilling out a whole crop of virus cells—each identical to the original invading virus and each in search of new body cells to invade.

Because their survival depends upon host cells, it is no coincidence that many viruses are highly contagious—in order to keep alive, they must constantly seek new hosts. Colds, for instance, easily spread from one person to another through hand-to-hand and hand-to-object contact, sneezes, and coughs. Unfortunately, of the 500 or more viruses that exist, few are killed by antibiotic drugs. Although some can be prevented by vaccines and some, like HIV, cause serious harm to the body, most viruses "run their course," invading the body, infecting body cells and tissues, and making us feel miserable. The course is run when—and if—the body's defensive system is able to destroy the virus.

OUR IMMUNE SYSTEM

Fortunately for us—given the countless number of harmful germs that exist in the world—the human body is well equipped to fight disease and infections. Our largest organ—the skin—provides the first line of defense by preventing germs from entering our body. (Open cuts and sores anywhere on our skin, however, can give invaders a direct route into our bloodstream.) In addition, our salty tears can wash away foreign substances, chemicals in our saliva can destroy them, and hair and mucus in our breathing passages and throat can trap and expel them.

If a foreign substance does manage to break through these barriers and enter our body, it triggers an immune response from special white blood cells, proteins, and chemicals that make up our immune system. Many parts of the body, including various glands, blood vessels, and vital organs play important roles in this complex system. Two kinds of white blood cells, the lymphocytes and the phagocytes, are especially critical to keeping our body free of infections and diseases. These white blood cells patrol the body, locate and identify enemies, destroy or neutralize invaders, and control the battle.

These cells can distinguish between healthy cells that belong in our body and disease-producing invaders or antigens such as bacteria and viruses. Every cell in our body is marked with a molecule on its surface that identifies itself as part of the body, a sort of friendly flag. Substances without a familiar flag are considered enemies. The job of the immune system is to identify and rid the body of enemies. When our immune cells find a substance without a friendly flag, they coordinate an elaborate attack to rid the body of this intruder. Any substance that is identified as an enemy and marked for expulsion, from a virus to a splinter, is called an antigen.

When an antigen is present in our body, our white blood cells multiply rapidly to wage an effective defense. They frequently release chemicals that cause inflammation and fever. These are uncomfortable symptoms for us, but they help fight infections by making it difficult for the germs to survive. These chemicals also draw the phagocytes to the scene. The macrophage (or "big-eater"), often the first to arrive, surrounds and engulfs or eats the enemy. Another kind of phagocyte that directly repels invaders is the granulocyte, which destroys itself even as it destroys the antigen.

The most important immune system cells are the B-cell and the T-cell lymphocytes. They are in charge of coordinating and regulating the daily battles our body wages against harmful viruses, bacteria, and other microbes. They provide protection or immunity against disease.

B-CELLS AND ANTIBODIES (HUMORAL IMMUNITY)

B-cells develop in bone marrow, the soft tissue inside our bones. These cells provide what scientists call humoral immunity. Alerted by the T-cells when an antigen is present, the B-cells produce special protein molecules called antibodies. Antibodies are custom-made for specific antigens. Like the pieces of a puzzle, the molecules of the antibody fit those—and only those—of the antigen. Antibodies help to fight infections by locking onto antigens, thereby immobilizing them and preventing them from attaching to healthy cells. After the antigen and antibody join, they can be found and eaten by macrophages.

When the immune system has successfully rid the body of the infection or disease, some of the B-cells become memory cells. These special cells, which are stored in the lymph nodes, will immediately "remember" or recognize this same antigen if it reinfects the body. They will produce the appropriate

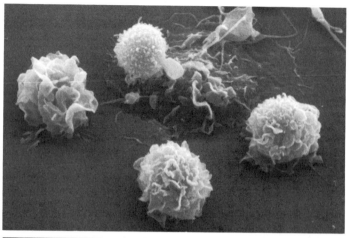

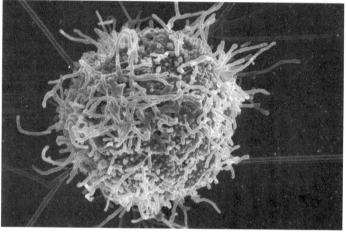

The electron micrograph at top shows healthy white bloods cells, magnified 9,000 times. The round T-cell at center, which is a lymphoctye, is adhered to a macrophage, a type of phagocyte. White blood cells fight infections and diseases that invade the body.

The T-cell in the micrograph at bottom, magnified 7,000 times, has been infected with HIV. Virus particles are attached to the cell surface.

antibodies to destroy the antigen so quickly that we will not even know we were infected with the germ. This is how the body builds up immunity, or protection, against certain diseases. It is also how a vaccination protects people from contracting many diseases, such as measles, some strains of the flu, and whooping cough. When you are given a vaccination for measles, for example, you are actually given a small dose of the measles virus. The amount of virus in a vaccine is not enough to make you sick, but is enough to cause the body to produce antibodies, which will spring into action should you come in contact with measles in the future.

T-CELLS (CELL-MEDIATED IMMUNITY)

T-cell lymphocytes develop in the thymus gland, a small organ located under the breastbone. The protection provided by these cells is called cell-mediated immunity. There are three main types of T-lymphocyte cells, each with a specific disease-fighting role.

Killer T-cells, as the name implies, directly attack and destroy virus-infected cells. They carry a molecule on their surfaces called a CD8 molecule and are also called killer T8 cells.

T-helper cells are lymphocytes that circulate throughout the body searching for foreign invaders and alert other immune cells if they find any antigens. One of their most important functions is to instruct the B-cells to make antibodies. T-helper cells carry a CD4 molecule on their surface and are also called T4 cells.

Suppressor T-cells are responsible for shutting off the immune system's response when the invader has been destroyed. This keeps the immune system from overreacting and destroying healthy cells. These cells also carry the CD8 molecule on their surface and are sometimes called suppressor T8 cells. The ratio between T-helper and T-suppressor cells is usually 2 to 1. People with AIDS often have this ratio reversed, which often causes allergic reactions, anemia, and cancers.

Able to fend off countless germs with amazing speed and efficiency, our immune system is truly a work of wonder. Although even the healthiest person can come down with an illness from time to time, the risk of infection is much greater when one's immune system is weak. Malnutrition, cancer, other infections, drugs, and even stress and depression can weaken this system, making us more vulnerable to infections. HIV makes a person particularly vulnerable to infections because this virus attacks and destroys the very cells designed to protect the body from disease.

Like other viruses, HIV infects various cells, organs, and tissues of the human body. Unlike any other virus, however, HIV primarily attacks and damages our T-cells, the masters of our immune system. It does this easily because its surface molecules, called gp-120, fit perfectly with CD4 molecules found on the surface of T4 cells. Other body cells have CD4 receptors as well, including macrophages and cells in the brain, lungs, and intestinal tract. Although HIV's chief targets are cells with these molecules, the virus also damages other cells, including suppressor T8 cells, which are responsible for calling off the immune system's response.

HIV: A RETROVIRUS

The way in which HIV reproduces is different from other viruses. HIV is a retrovirus, a rare virus whose instructions for reproduction are carried in strands of RNA (ribonucleic acid). Most other viruses, as well as body cells, carry their genetic material in strands of DNA. Normally, a body cell would not recognize instructions for duplication written on a strand of RNA. HIV, however, contains a special enzyme called reverse transcriptase that converts its RNA into DNA, the genetic code that our body cell recognizes. Once infected, the host cell reads the virus's new DNA strands as its own and begins to replicate the virus. Two other virus enzymes, called protease and integrase, help HIV complete this process. Soon the healthy cell is full of viruses. The cell bursts open and releases these new viruses, which then search for new cells to infect. The more T-cells that are damaged or destroyed, the fewer resources the body has to mount a defense against other diseases.

Scientists do not entirely understand why our immune system does not destroy HIV before it does so much damage. Interestingly, when HIV invades the body, our immune system appears to respond as it normally would to the presence of an infection: Lymphocytes multiply and HIV antibodies are manufactured. This response, however, is not strong enough to rid the body of HIV. Although no one is certain at this time, it appears that HIV invades cells so rapidly that HIV antibodies are not sufficient to defeat the virus. Antibodies cannot enter body cells, so once inside a host cell the virus is safe from their attack. Another reason that HIV gains such a strong foothold so quickly may be related to its uncanny ability to mutate or change its form. If a virus changes, even slightly, antibodies do not recognize this new form of virus.

FROM HIV INFECTION TO AIDS

Stage 1: Some people experience a few days of flu-like symptoms within weeks of being infected by HIV, but most people experience no symptoms at all for many years. People who are infected but have no symptoms are said to be asymptomatic (without symptoms). An asymptomatic person is still infected with HIV and can still infect others. This stage can last from two years to more than ten years.

Stage 2: The earliest signs of HIV infection are fevers, weight loss of more than 10 pounds (4.5 kilograms), swollen glands, frequent yeast infections, night sweats, diarrhea, fatigue, and skin rashes. These are also the signs of many other illnesses, such as the flu or another virus, and do not necessarily mean that a person is infected with HIV. If the symptoms are severe, unexplainable, and last for a long time, it would be wise to see a doctor. These are often the earliest signs that the immune system is being challenged by HIV. This stage can last from a few months to many years.

Stage 3: As the immune system weakens, more serious infections and diseases appear. Illnesses that indicate that the immune system is failing include thrush (a fungal infection of the mouth, esophagus, and vagina) and shingles (a painful herpes virus).

AIDS

Stage 4: The immune system is no longer able to combat infections. According to guidelines established by the CDC, a person with AIDS has a CD4 count below 200 (normal range is 600–1500 per cubic millimeter of blood) and/or one or more of about twenty-six opportunistic infections.

Many AIDS-related infections stem from various protozoans, parasites, bacteria, and viruses that are already in the body. The most common include:

Pneumocystis carinii pneumonia (PCP), a rare lung infection caused by a protozoan parasite.

Primary brain lymphoma, a rare brain cancer.

Cytomegalovirus disease (CMV), a herpes virus that damages the eyes, colon, lungs, and brain.

Toxoplasmosis of the brain, an infection of the central nervous system caused by a protozoan found in cats, uncooked meat, and unpasteurized milk.

In 1993 the CDC added invasive cervical cancer, pulmonary tuberculosis, and recurrent pneumonia to its list of AIDS-defining diseases.

HIV infection and AIDS are very dangerous, frightening conditions. Although early treatment of opportunistic infections can help people with AIDS live for many years, AIDS is still a deadly disease. It is not known whether everyone who is infected with HIV will develop AIDS, but doctors generally agree that HIV is a lifelong infection that constantly challenges and threatens the body's ability to fight other infections and diseases. Fortunately, HIV is not an easy virus to get. Unlike most other germs, this virus does not survive in the air we breathe, in the water we drink, or on objects we touch. As we will see in the next chapter, it is passed from one person to another through very intimate, not casual or day-to-day, contact.

3

HIV Transmission

HIV is not spread through casual contact. HIV is not easy to contract. People don't "catch" HIV or AIDS from others in the same ways they might catch other infections. Compared with most other germs in the world, HIV does not spread from one person to another very easily. Because the virus is quite fragile:

- HIV cannot survive in the air or in water. You can't get it by breathing the same air, swimming in the same pool, or drinking from the same glass as someone who is infected with HIV.
- HIV cannot live on objects. You can't get it from toilet seats, water fountains, utensils, or telephones.
- HIV is not carried by mosquitoes, ticks, or insects. Even if a mosquito were to bite an HIV-infected person, there would not be enough infected blood in the mosquito to infect anyone else. One government study estimated that it would take about 3,000 bites from an HIV-infected mosquito to pose any kind of threat to a person.[1]
- Although HIV is present in saliva, doctors do not believe there is enough virus in saliva to cause infection. So far, there has not been a documented case of a person contracting HIV as a result of being coughed on, spit at, or kissed by an HIV-infected person.

This is the way many people deal with HIV.

A lot of people don't think they have to worry about HIV. But the truth is, anyone can get HIV infection if they are sharing drug needles and syringes or having sex with an infected person. Call your State or local AIDS hotline. Or call the National AIDS Hotline at 1-800-342-AIDS. Call 1-800-243-7889 (TTY) for deaf access.

CDC U.S. DEPARTMENT OF HEALTH AND HUMAN SERVICES
Public Health Service
Centers for Disease Control

 HIV is the virus that causes AIDS.

AMERICA RESPONDS TO AIDS

HOW HIV IS SPREAD

Many germs, like those that cause the flu and strep throat, infect the lungs, throat, and sinuses. They can be spread when coughs and sneezes expel the virus into the air, onto objects you might touch, or onto your hands and other parts of the body. HIV, on the other hand, primarily infects lymphocytes, the white blood cells responsible for fighting infections. HIV can therefore be found in body fluids that contain lymphocytes.

In order to become infected with the AIDS virus, you must come in direct contact with infected body fluids. Some fluids, like tears and saliva, don't carry enough viruses to infect another person, and some, like those in the brain, are not the kind another person would ever encounter. HIV is transmitted from one person to another through direct contact with the semen, vaginal secretions, and blood of an infected person.

The way a person could come in contact with these fluids is through sexual activity, sharing of intravenous needles, and exposure to contaminated blood during childbirth, transfusions, or other medical procedures. Although the instances have been rare, infants can be infected through a mother's breast milk.

SEXUAL TRANSMISSION

HIV is a sexually transmitted disease. This means that it can be transmitted to another person when HIV-infected semen or vaginal secretions are exchanged during sexual activity.

HIV can be passed from a man to a woman or from a woman to a man during sex. This is called heterosexual transmission. This usually happens during vaginal intercourse, when a man inserts his penis and ejects semen (ejaculates) inside a woman's vagina.

If the man is HIV-infected, the virus in his semen can infect immune cells present in the woman's vagina and vaginal fluids. HIV also can penetrate the tissues of skin that line the inside of the vagina (called mucous membranes) and enter the bloodstream. Developing young teenage girls are particularly vulnerable to this type of transmission because these tissues are especially thin. A cut, sore, or even a microscopic tear in the vaginal tissues provide a direct route for HIV into the body and the bloodstream.

If a woman is HIV-infected, the virus is present in the cells of the fluids or secretions in her vagina. These fluids can enter the man's bloodstream through the small opening of the urethra, the tube inside the penis that carries semen and urine from the body, and infect immune cells in the mucous membranes that line this tube. Cuts, abrasions, or sores on the penis itself increase the chance of the man's becoming infected.

The percentage of people with AIDS who contracted HIV through heterosexual contact increased from 1.9 percent in 1985 to 10 percent in 1995.

Both men and women can become infected with HIV through vaginal intercourse. Women, however, are at least twice as likely to be infected this way. There are several reasons for this. First, far more viruses are present in semen than in vaginal fluids. Second, semen stays in the vagina after intercourse, so women are exposed to the virus for a longer time than men. Third, the walls of the vagina cover more surface area than the urethra's small opening at the tip of the penis, giving the virus more opportunity to infect cells or enter the bloodstream. Despite these differences, both men and women can contract HIV from unprotected vaginal intercourse with an infected partner.

Anal Intercourse

HIV can also be transmitted through anal, or rectal, intercourse, in which a man, called the insertive partner, inserts his penis and ejaculates inside the rectum of another person, called the receptive partner. If the insertive partner is infected, the virus in his semen can penetrate the receptive partner's tissues and infect immune cells, especially those in the large intestine. HIV is spread very easily during anal intercourse because the tissues or membranes inside the rectum are very thin. Moreover, these membranes can tear easily, even bleed, during this kind of sexual activity, providing a direct pathway into the bloodstream. Because bleeding is likely during this kind of sex, the receptive partner is at a greater risk for infection, just as the woman is during vaginal sex. There is, however, still a risk to the insertive partner as well. HIV-infected blood, or even feces, inside the rectum can enter the urethra or any cuts on the penis.

Because anal sex is one of the main ways that men have sex with other men, it is the most common way that homosexual and bisexual men become infected with HIV. Anal intercourse, however, is not exclusively a gay activity. Many heterosexual or "straight" couples have tried or regularly engage in anal sex as well. Some young people apparently have anal sex to avoid pregnancy or to "hold on" to their virginity. It is the activity that is risky, not a person's gender or sexual orientation (gay or straight). Anal sex is a risky sexual behavior for both men and women.

Oral Sex

During oral sex, a person uses his or her mouth and/or tongue to stimulate a partner's sex organs. Experts caution that it may be possible for infected semen or vaginal fluids to infect cells in the mouth or throat, especially if there are any cuts or sores present. In addition, HIV-infected menstrual blood or blood from mouth sores or a gum infection could conceivably infect another person. Although studies suggest that saliva contains a chemical that inactivates HIV, no one knows for sure if oral sex can transmit the AIDS virus. The risk is probably quite low, but unprotected oral sex still should be regarded as a possible way to contract HIV.

Kissing

Kissing is not a risky activity. Even french kissing is considered relatively safe because saliva contains so few viruses. If, however, infected blood is present in the mouth and is exchanged with a partner who has sores in his or her mouth, it is possible that HIV could enter the partner's bloodstream.

To contract HIV sexually, semen, vaginal secretions, or blood must enter a pathway into the bloodstream. The penis, vagina, or anus are the most common routes for HIV infection, but broken skin on hands or other parts of the body can also provide a pathway for the virus.

BLOOD-TO-BLOOD TRANSMISSION

Direct contact with HIV-infected blood is another way that HIV is transmitted from one person to another. This kind of transmission can occur in several ways, but the most common is by using infected needles and syringes to inject drugs. About 27 percent of the people in the United States diagnosed with AIDS in 1995 contracted the virus through contaminated equipment used to inject or shoot drugs.

Injection Drug Use (IDU)

An estimated 1.2 million people in the United States inject illegal drugs. Some are occasional or recreational users, but many buy and use them everyday because they are physically dependent or addicted. The equipment used to inject drugs includes a needle and syringe, called a set, works, or a set of works. Except if prescribed by a doctor for medical reasons, it is generally illegal to possess this equipment in the

United States. Because needles are scarce, many injection drug users share them with other users or pay to use them.

Sharing needles is very dangerous. Works and other paraphernalia, including containers to mix the drug powder with water so it can be drawn through the needle and into the syringe, can contain HIV-infected blood from previous users. This occurs because there is always some blood or tissue that comes back into the syringe after a person shoots drugs into a vein or the skin. If this blood is infected with HIV, whoever uses this equipment unknowingly mixes the infected blood, which is not always visible, with the drug solution and shoots it directly into his or her own bloodstream.

In some cities in the United States, more than half of the people who use injection drugs are infected with HIV. Anyone who uses another person's works to inject drugs runs a great risk of becoming infected with the AIDS virus. You cannot tell who is infected or whether the needle being used is clean. Most people use needles to inject illegal drugs like cocaine, heroin, and speed, but some people also inject other substances like steroids and vitamins. The type of substance has nothing to do with HIV. It is not the drug that carries the virus, but the injection equipment.

AIDS

In 1995 almost half of the women with AIDS in the United States were infected with HIV through injection drug use.

Injection drug use is the principal way that women in the United States become infected with the AIDS virus. Nearly half—about 41 percent—of women with AIDS were infected with HIV through contaminated needles used to shoot drugs, and experts believe that sexual contact with an injection drug user accounts for the majority of women who contracted the virus from sexual contact. Thus, injection drug use accounts, directly or indirectly, for most AIDS cases among American women.

MOTHER-TO-CHILD TRANSMISSION

The AIDS virus can be transmitted from an HIV-infected mother to a child during pregnancy and delivery. During pregnancy, the virus can pass through the placenta, the barrier designed to protect babies from diseases while they are in the womb. HIV infection also can occur during delivery because the baby may come in contact with the mother's blood in the birth canal. Not all babies whose mothers have the AIDS virus will contract HIV, but about one in four will. Doctors do not fully understand why this is so and are studying whether other factors might affect the risk of infection. It is possible, for instance, that the stage of the mother's infection or the amount of virus in her bloodstream may contribute to this kind of transmission in some way.

Hundreds of thousands of infants throughout the world are born infected with HIV each year. Their future is uncertain. Although some, especially those fortunate enough to live in countries with good medical care, may reach their teens, most become sick and die before the age of five.

In 1995 about 200,000 infants in the world contracted HIV from their mothers. About 2,000
infants in the United States contracted HIV
this way.

Until now, doctors could do very little to change the
course of infection of an unborn child. The results of
a recent study of infected pregnant women and their
children, however, are promising. This study found
that the risk of this kind of transmission can be significantly reduced—from about 25 percent to about
8 percent—by giving a drug called AZT (azidothymidine) to HIV-infected mothers during pregnancy and
delivery and to the infants immediately after birth.
Doctors are hopeful that this and similar drugs will
help prevent children from contracting HIV in the
future.

Blood Transfusions

Blood and blood products used for transfusions and
treatment of blood disorders like hemophilia come
from volunteers who donate blood. If a person who
donates blood is infected with a disease, the person
who receives the blood can become infected with the
disease. Before 1985, when a test was developed to
detect HIV in blood, thousands of people in the
United States were infected with HIV because they
received blood from donors who were infected. Ryan
White, for instance, was infected through contaminated blood products he infused to treat his hemo-

philia. In 1992 the world was stunned to learn that Arthur Ashe, the tennis champion, had been infected with HIV through a blood transfusion he received during a heart operation in 1983.

Today the blood supply in the United States is quite safe. Blood-banking organizations like the Red Cross carefully screen people who wish to donate blood. Applicants must fill out a detailed questionnaire about their past and present sexual behavior and drug use. Those who indicate that they have engaged in high-risk behaviors are not allowed to donate blood. This includes gay and bisexual men who have had numerous sex partners, as well as anyone who has engaged in prostitution, has injected drugs, or has sex with a partner who is at risk for HIV. Of course, this procedure does not eliminate every person who is infected. Not all people are aware of all of their risk factors, and not all tell the truth about their sexual behavior and drug use. As a result, experts estimate that about 1,000 people with HIV donate blood every year.[2]

After blood has been donated, it is tested for evidence of various diseases, including HIV. The test for HIV, discussed in Chapter 7, looks for HIV antibodies rather than the actual virus. If HIV antibodies are found, the blood is treated to destroy the virus and then is thrown away. Sometimes antibodies are not found in blood that is actually infected with HIV. This may happen because it can take several weeks or longer for HIV antibodies to show up in blood. So, if a person was only recently infected, his or her blood might be free of HIV antibodies but still infected with HIV. Even though HIV antibody tests are not 100 percent accurate, the current risk of infection through transfusion is still very low. In fact, the Centers for Disease Control and Prevention (CDC) estimates this risk to be from about 1 in 39,000 to 1 in 250,000.[3] More accurate tests may be developed in the future, which could result in the complete elimination of this kind of transmission.

Health-Care Providers

"Accidents do happen on the job," says Lu-Anne, an HIV nurse practitioner. "I can't tell you how many times I've been stuck by a needle and splashed with blood and pus during my years of nursing. These are never very pleasant experiences, but HIV has made them much worse. I've been stuck twice now by needles that contain the blood of HIV patients. Both times, even though I knew there was only a slim chance I could be infected, I was absolutely terrified. Both times, thankfully, I tested negative for HIV. I'm as careful as I can be, but I just can't worry about it all the time. I love my work and my patients too much to be afraid."

Health-care providers and other caretakers come in contact with blood and body fluids every day when they draw blood, clean wounds, and perform other medical procedures. To protect themselves from infections and injuries, they use "universal precautions" when caring for all patients. These safety measures include wearing protective glasses and gloves, as well as careful handling and disposal of all needles, blood, and body fluids. Other professionals, such as police, fire fighters, funeral workers, and prison officials, also use these same precautions. As a result of these safety procedures, only a very small number of medical workers have become infected with HIV from the blood or other body fluid of patients.

ADDITIONAL FACTORS

Not everyone who is exposed to HIV becomes infected with the virus. The number of times a person is exposed to the virus can increase the chances of infection, but even some longtime partners of HIV-infected people have escaped infection. Magic Johnson's wife, for instance, was pregnant with their first child when he announced his infection. She, and later their son, tested negative for HIV.

Experts are not sure why some people contract the virus and others do not, but they suspect that there may be other factors that play a role in transmission. It is possible, for instance, that some strains of HIV transmit the virus more easily than other strains.

AIDS

"Neither dentist would see me, due to HIV infection. One dentist told me that his office was carpeted and he would not be able to sterilize the room after my visit. A second dentist told me she had plants and could not take the risk of my infecting her plants and then infecting her other patients."

Ronald Jerrell, July 1990
America Living with AIDS

It is also possible that the virus is more infectious during certain stages of infection. Perhaps some people are able to fight off the virus before it infects cells. These theories are still being researched.

What experts do know is that the presence of other infections in the body can increase the risk of HIV infection. When you are fighting any kind of infection, your immune system is working at full speed to rid the body of these germs and is less able to fight other germs. As you know, the white blood cells of the immune system multiply when an infection is present. Not only are these cells then less able to mount a defense against HIV, but their large numbers give the virus even more cells to infect. If the infection is another sexually transmitted disease, there are millions of white blood cells at the scene of the infection—the anus, the vagina, and the penis. In addition, and perhaps most important, STDs often cause tissue tenderness, blisters, open sores, and scabs. A person with genital sores, for example, is more likely to contract HIV.

The number of people in the United States with STDs has increased dramatically. Persons who are sexually active are at high risk for contracting this kind of infection.

PROTECTING YOURSELF

AIDS is not about "us" and "them." People don't get HIV because they're "bad" and people are not protected because they're "good." You don't get HIV because of who you are—you get it because of what you do.
—Magic Johnson[4]

The facts about HIV and sex are clear: Unprotected sexual intercourse is risky. You cannot tell who is infected and who is not. The person you are involved with may be carrying the virus and could give it to you. Your partner may not know he or she is infected. Protecting yourself and your sex partners is your responsibility.

The link between HIV and drugs is also clear: Sharing needles to inject drugs transmits the AIDS virus. People who share needles with an HIV-infected person can become infected, and sexual partners of HIV-infected drug users can become infected. They, in turn, can infect other sexual partners.

Injection drugs are the most obvious link between HIV and drugs, but the use of alcohol, cocaine, crack, and other drugs is also risky. Not only do these substances cause emotional and physical damage, but they also impair judgment. People who drink too much or get "high" are more likely to have sex, as well as to "forget" to protect themselves during sex. Crack cocaine is strongly associated with HIV because people are so quickly addicted to this drug. Many can't afford to buy crack and resort to trading sex for money to get it. Sex with multiple partners, of course, is a high-risk behavior for contracting HIV.

Without a doubt, AIDS has affected the way we think about and approach romantic relationships, dating, and sex. HIV is, after all, a potentially fatal infection that can be transmitted sexually. It is best to remember that, as frightening as it is, HIV is a virus that is preventable. There are many ways that you can protect yourself from infection—without giving up a physical relationship. In Chapter 4, you will learn how to reduce your risk of HIV infection.

4

Reducing the Risk of Infection

HIV INFECTIONS AMONG WOMEN
AND TEENS ARE INCREASING

ANTIVIRAL DRUGS FAIL TO HALT ONSET OF AIDS

NO CURE FOR AIDS YET

AIDS VACCINE STILL YEARS AWAY

For more than a decade, our newspapers have been filled with depressing and frightening news stories about HIV infection and AIDS. As the number of deaths from AIDS and the number of HIV infections multiply, it is hard to find many encouraging reports about this new and dangerous virus. The following headlines, equally true, illustrate that we already have the power to stop the spread of AIDS in our country:

HIV CAN BE PREVENTED

CONDOMS SIGNIFICANTLY REDUCE RISK OF HIV

MORE TEENS CHOOSING ABSTINENCE

NEEDLE EXCHANGE PROGRAMS REDUCE
NUMBER OF NEW HIV INFECTIONS

As scientists study this virus and researchers experiment with drugs and preventive vaccines, AIDS educators stress that HIV is preventable. If you know how to prevent HIV, you can change your behavior so that you won't have to worry about contracting this virus. You already know that HIV infection requires the exchange of body fluids. The two ways to avoid this virus are simple: Always practice safe sex, and never inject drugs or share needles. To reduce your risk of infection, you must always practice safer sex, and use bleach to clean needles if you inject drugs.

SAFE SEX: ABSTINENCE

For some kids, sex is no big deal. They see it as just something you do when you go out with someone. I know a lot of young girls who are having sex, not because they really want to, but because they think it's expected of them. Well, I do think sex is a big deal, so I'm waiting until I'm older and more together to have that intense a relationship. There's nothing wrong with waiting—it doesn't mean you're immature or a prude. And I've found that plenty of boys are relieved to just relax and have fun without getting into a real heavy thing. I've had a great time in school and have made lots of really good friends. I tell the younger people I counsel that I haven't missed a thing —except maybe getting hurt, getting pregnant, or getting AIDS.
—Julie, age 17

Julie, a high school senior who helps lead HIV prevention workshops at local middle and high schools in her community, has decided to wait until she is older to have a sexual relationship. She knows not only a lot about AIDS, but also a lot about herself and what she wants in life. She thinks that sex should be a special part of a trusting and committed long-term relationship. She also knows that the only way she can be 100 percent sure she will not get this virus through sexual contact is if she does not have sexual intercourse. She is practicing the only safe sex there is today: abstinence.

Sexual abstinence means refraining from sexual intercourse. Current statistics show that as many as half of all high school students are sexually active. It stands to reason, then, that an equal percentage are abstaining from sex. Many are consciously choosing to wait until they are older to have sex. Whether it is based on moral, religious, health, or other personal reasons, this decision is not always easy—especially for young people whose friends already are sexually active or whose partners want to have sex. Yet another pressure comes from our culture. Popular music, music videos, TV shows, movies, and even commercials bombard us with sexual images every day. The message seems to be: Just do it. But just doing it is risky.

AIDS

The World Health Organization estimates that at least half of the people in the world who have AIDS were infected with HIV during their adolescence.

If you abstain from sexual intercourse, you cannot contract AIDS through sex. You can still have a very passionate physical relationship with your partner—probably one that is even more intimate than intercourse is for most young people. Kissing, hugging, body massage and rubbing, and masturbation are HIV-safe activities. They keep you safe from pregnancy, HIV, and other STDs, and allow you to experience a mutually satisfying sexual relationship. Always be careful, however, that fluids—semen and vaginal secretions—do not enter the body or contact broken skin.

Practicing safe sex requires a little imagination and a lot of self-control. If you and your partner have decided to wait to have intercourse, keep yourselves safe by avoiding activities or situations that weaken your resolve to stay safe. It is not wise, for instance, to spend a lot of unsupervised time together. Mixing drugs and alcohol with sex is especially risky because these substances affect your thinking, your judgment, and your behavior.

SAFER SEX

If you do have sexual intercourse, you can reduce your risk of contracting HIV by practicing safer sex. To practice safer sex you must use a latex condom every time you have oral, anal, or vaginal sex. Condoms or "rubbers" are protective covers that fit over the penis. They prevent pregnancy and many sexually transmitted diseases, including HIV, by trapping semen inside the condom. The man wearing the condom is also protected against HIV and other STDs.

When used correctly, condoms prevent pregnancy and disease. When used correctly and every time you have sex, condoms offer sexually active people the best available protection against HIV. Although studies show that condom failure is unlikely if they are used properly, condoms can break or slip off. Here are some simple rules to help you use condoms correctly so you can protect yourself from infection.

- Always use a latex condom, never one made of animal skin or other natural substances.
- Check the expiration date printed on the outside of the condom package. Don't buy or use a condom if that date has passed.
- Store condoms in a cool, dry place. A wallet is probably fine for a day or two, and you should keep a supply handy, but it's not a good idea to use your wallet as a long-term storage place.
- Most condoms are lubricated. If extra lubrication is needed or desired, only use water-based products such as K.Y. Jelly, Cornhusker's Lotion, or H-R Jelly. Do not use lubricants that contain oil, such as Vaseline, baby oil, or mineral oil, because they can weaken the condom and increase the chance that it might break.
- For extra protection, most doctors recommend that you use a spermicide, a chemical that kills sperm, called nonoxynol-9, with a condom. You can buy condoms that contain nonoxynol-9. This type of spermicide is also found in a variety of birth-control foams, creams, jellies, and sponges, which are inserted before inter-

Volunteers load condoms and leaflets into bags that they will distribute on the streets of New York City to promote safer sex and AIDS awareness.

course. Read the product's instruction to know when you can insert them and when you should remove them after sex. Spermicide alone is not adequate protection against HIV—you must use a condom and the spermicide together.
- Put on and take off condoms carefully. Always put the condom on when the penis is erect, but before intercourse. Roll the condom over the penis, leaving about one-half inch at the tip to "catch" the semen after ejaculation.
- To prevent the condom from slipping off or leaking, the man wearing the condom should press the rim of the condom against the penis and withdraw immediately after ejaculation (while the penis is still erect).
- Throw used condoms away. Use a new condom each time you have intercourse.

These steps may sound complicated, and most people do fumble at first, which might be awkward or embarrassing. No one is an instant expert. With practice and experience, you will find condoms easy to use. They are also easy to buy. You can buy them in drugstores, as well as in many grocery stores and vending machines in restrooms. You don't need a doctor's prescription or your parents' permission, and, in most places, they are displayed on the counter so you often do not even have to ask for them. Millions of people buy condoms every day, and salespeople are used to selling them.

Other kinds of condoms and barrier devices help prevent the spread of HIV. Dental dams are plastic barriers that protect the mouth from contact with body fluids. They are recommended for use during oral sex. In addition, the new female condom, approved by the Federal Drug Administration in 1993, gives women the ability to protect themselves rather than rely on their male partner's cooperation. This is a protective sheath that covers the cervix, as well as both the inside and outside of the vagina. Most experts agree that the female condoms available in the United States represent a major step forward, but warn that they are not as effective in HIV protection as the male condom. Researchers hope that more effective and easy-to-use female condoms will be available to women in the near future.

THEY ONLY WORK IF YOU USE THEM

Condoms only work if you use them. If condoms are so easy to use and provide good protection against HIV, why doesn't every sexually active person use them? This is a question that AIDS educators have been asking for years, but, unfortunately, there is no simple answer.

Although an increasing number of women are insisting on safer sex, it is still the male who ultimately decides whether condoms are used during sex. Despite overwhelming evidence that condoms help protect against HIV, many young and even adult men are still reluctant to use them. Some are unwilling because they think that condoms will interfere with their sexual pleasure; some do not understand the risks of unprotected sex; and some apparently are willing to take their chances of contracting HIV or other sexually transmitted diseases.

Overcoming resistance to using condoms can be tricky, but if you have unprotected sex—sexual intercourse without a condom—you are putting yourself at risk for HIV. Both partners in a sexual relationship are responsible for protecting themselves. The first step is for them to discuss safer sex.

Talking about HIV prevention and safer sex is a necessary part of a responsible sexual relationship. This discussion must include possible risk factors, such as your and your partner's past sexual and drug history, and how to have safe and safer sex. This may seem very unromantic and even embarrassing, but a few uncomfortable moments is a small price to pay for a healthy life. If you cannot even imagine having this kind of conversation with your partner, perhaps you should take a few steps back and think about whether you should be having sex or considering having sex.

Some people find that practicing ahead of time helps them get over their shyness about discussing HIV and safer sex. In fact, many sex education and health classes in public schools are helping young people find comfortable ways to talk about these issues through role-playing sessions. If your school does not offer this kind of support, you could get together with friends, discuss why safer sex is important to you, and think of ways you could communicate your feelings to your partner. You might want to brush up on the information you have learned about AIDS, as well as to think about your reaction to such standard lines as "Don't you trust me?" or "You must not really care about me." Role-playing may make you a little more secure and determined, but remember that this is not a debating contest. You have the right to insist on safer sex.

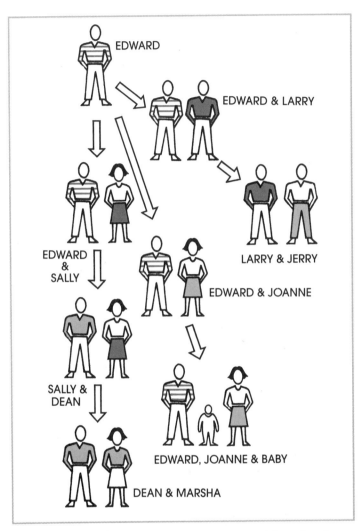

One person infected with HIV can spread the virus to many others by engaging in risky behavior. HIV is transmitted from one person to another through direct contact with the semen, vaginal secretions, or blood of an infected person. (Adapted from *What You Can Do to Avoid AIDS* by Magic Johnson.)

LIMIT THE NUMBER OF
SEXUAL PARTNERS

Young people are rarely ready to settle down with one person in a long-term relationship. If you are a normal teenager, you probably will fall in and out of love many times before you make a lifelong or even a long-term commitment to someone. If you include sexual intercourse in all of these relationships, you will end up having sex with many people. If you limit the number of your sexual partners, you will reduce your risks of having sex with someone who is infected with HIV. You may also increase your chances of finding someone special, someone with whom you might develop a trusting and long-term relationship. So take your time!

Knowing someone well, regardless of how terrific he or she is, is no substitute for safer sex. Few HIV-infected teens are even aware that they are infected. If you and your partner do decide to have sex, have an HIV antibody test to determine if either one of you has been infected. (This test, discussed in Chapter 6, is especially recommended for couples who are thinking about having a child together.)

Safe-sex and safer-sex behavior provide excellent protection against HIV. If you follow the guidelines discussed in this section, you will significantly reduce your risks of contracting HIV through sexual activity.

If you abstain from sexual intercourse, you cannot contract AIDS through sex.

PREVENTING HIV TRANSMISSION
THROUGH INJECTION DRUG USE

An ever-increasing number of Americans are now contracting HIV from contaminated needles they use to inject drugs. People who are infected this way can spread HIV to other drug users who share their injection equipment, as well as to sexual partners. Women can pass on the virus to their unborn children.

- If you never inject drugs, you will never contract HIV this way. (You must, of course, still protect yourself from getting the virus through sexual contact.) If you don't use these drugs or needles, don't start. The needles as well as the injection drugs—like cocaine, heroin, and amphetamines (speed)—can be deadly.
- If you inject drugs, you are at high risk for HIV infection, as well as for drug addiction and drug overdose. If you are a casual user, you can avoid a life of addiction, disease, and, quite possibly, early death by changing your behavior now. In order to accomplish this goal, you may have to stop hanging out with friends who use drugs, find new activities to occupy your time, and get counseling and extra support to help you stick with your decision.
- If you use injection drugs regularly, you are at serious risk for HIV infection, as well as other dangerous blood-borne diseases such as hepatitis. It is never too late to stop shooting or using drugs. You can save your own and other people's lives by getting help to stop your drug use. Drug addiction is a serious disease, and, like alcoholism, not always easy to quit.

Although some drug addicts can quit on their own, most need support and treatment at either an out-patient clinic or a residential facility. Unfortunately, not enough drug treatment centers are available to serve all the people who want to quit their drug habits. You may find a waiting list for treatment, but if you are now using drugs and want to stop, get the help you need. The drug agencies listed in the Sources section of this book can start you on the road to treatment and recovery.

In the meantime, do not share your equipment or use anyone else's equipment to shoot drugs. New, sterile needles are hard to find, but about forty cities in the United States provide free, new needles and syringes to drug users.

Clean-needle exchange programs are still politically controversial, but they do significantly reduce HIV infection among IDUs. Check with your state public-health department to see if such a program exists in your area.

- If you can't stop injecting drugs and are sharing needles, the only way you can possibly reduce your risk of HIV infection is to clean your equipment—the needle and syringe—with chlorine bleach before and after use. Draw the bleach through the needle and into the syringe and then flush the bleach out through the needle into a container. Do this twice with the bleach and twice with clean water. This is the only method that can kill HIV in needles and syringes. Boiling equipment in water or simply heating the needle with a match will not kill the virus.

In 1995 nearly one-third of the people diagnosed with AIDS in the United States contracted HIV through infected needles and
syringes.

ANOTHER WAY THAT DRUGS CAN KILL

Injection drug use is one way that drugs can harm or
even kill you, but other drugs, researchers are finding, are just as deadly. Crack, a highly addictive form
of cocaine that is heated and smoked, is considered a
major cause of HIV infections among teens and
young adults. Crack is a stimulant that strips away
sexual inhibitions, often leading to frequent, unprotected sex. This drug also is linked with sex and HIV
in another crucial way. Crack users are quickly addicted to this drug and often trade sex for the drug or
for the money to buy it. This kind of commercial sex
rarely includes protection and often involves partners
who are also drug users, whose rates of HIV infection
are high. Until our society addresses the drug epidemic in our country, substance abuse will continue
to cause HIV infections among drug users, their sexual partners, and their children.

TEENS AND HIV

Adolescence is an exciting and busy time of life, and
most teenagers are deeply involved in school, sports,
music, dating, friends, and family. Adolescence is
also a time for experimentation, testing the limits,

and risk-taking. This has been true for generations, and parents and educators have worried about teenagers and their behavior for just as long. Most teens manage to make it through these difficult years safely. AIDS and STDs, however, make even healthy adolescent experimentation dangerous. Teenagers and young adults are contracting HIV at alarming, ever-increasing rates.

Millions of teenagers and young adults throughout the world are at risk for HIV infection. These at-risk teens often live in conditions of extreme deprivation, despair, and disorder. Many have been neglected or physically or sexually abused. Others have been rejected by their families because of their sexual preference or lifestyle. Some are throwaways—children whose parents and communities have given them up to the streets—and some are runaways— young people who have escaped to the streets. Because their expectations for the future are so low, they often feel they have nothing to gain and nothing to lose, and their chances of contracting HIV are especially great. Chapter 5 discusses why young people are at such risk of contracting HIV.

5

Teens and HIV:
Modern Romance, Modern Risks

*Everyone keeps talking about AIDS and
how all these teenagers are getting it now.
I guess that's happening in some places in
the world, but not in my town. I know a
lot of kids are getting infected with HIV,
but that's not something you can see or
feel. If it's not right in front of you, it's
hard to believe it's real.*
                                    —*Anne, age 16*

Every day young people all over the country—in
cities, towns, and rural communities—are getting together with friends, meeting new people, flirting, dating, and falling in and out of love. For most teenagers, regardless of their sexual orientation, physical
attraction and sexual activity are integral parts of romantic relationships. As carefree as they may appear,
young adults are aware of the risks inherent in modern romance—getting too involved, getting hurt, and
getting rejected. If they are having sex, there are additional risks—greater heartbreak, pregnancy, sexually
transmitted diseases, and AIDS. Although most know
these dangers exist, many young adults do not believe
that they are at risk.

Anne, a high school student in a large, suburban
town, is learning about AIDS in health classes in
school and has started to do research about the sub-

ject for a school report. Most kids, she says, know that HIV is a silent infection, but being aware of HIV and how the virus is transmitted does not always translate into safe behavior. "Even though we know the facts about things like drinking and driving, and unprotected sex and AIDS, most kids just never think anything bad is going to happen to them. Besides, it's hard to imagine that something you do now could show up and kill you ten years later," Anne says. "Ten years is like an eternity for us."

RISKY BEHAVIOR

As Anne points out, young people often feel that they are somehow protected from the dangers around them and from their own "living on the edge" behavior. Despite warnings from parents and educators, teenagers and young adults often behave recklessly—they drive too fast, ride in cars without seat belts or on bikes and motorcycles without helmets, and experiment with drugs and alcohol. All of these activities can cause serious harm, even death. Another risky behavior is related to sexual activity. Despite warnings about HIV, STDs, and unplanned pregnancy, more than half of sexually active teens have had unprotected sex. Young people who take such risks are putting their lives in danger.

AIDS

"I just didn't think it could happen to me."
Magic Johnson
What You Can Do to Avoid Aids

There are about 28 million teenagers in the United States. Here are some reasons that they are at risk for contracting HIV:

- Sexual activity: More than half of all teenagers have sexual intercourse by the time they are seventeen years old. By age twenty, 80 percent of males and 70 percent of females are sexually active.
- Unprotected sex: Sexually active teenagers do not practice safer sex consistently. Studies show that fewer than half consistently use condoms during sex.
- Risky sex: About one-quarter of all teens, male and female, report having had anal intercourse. This is a very risky sexual activity.
- Multiple partners: More than half of sexually active teens report having had two or more sexual partners.
- STDs: Sexually transmitted diseases are spread through unprotected sex. About 3 million adolescents contract an STD each year. The majority have no symptoms of infection.
- Male-male sex: One in every six teenage males has had one or more sexual encounters with another male. Some, but certainly not all, of these boys are or will be exclusively homosexual.
- Prostitution and survival sex: Between 90,000 and 300,000 teenage men and women trade sex for money or drugs.
- Drug and alcohol use: Almost half of high school seniors have tried illegal drugs, and 90 percent have used alcohol. Drugs and alcohol impair judgment, increase sexual activity, and decrease the use of condoms.

HIV INFECTION RATES

Anne was also right about the small number of teen-agers with AIDS. Teens with AIDS account for only about one percent of all the AIDS cases in the United States. This is not surprising, given the number of years between HIV infection and AIDS. Although the number of teens with full-blown AIDS is relatively low, the number of teens infected with HIV is not.

No one knows for sure just how many teenagers in this country are infected with HIV. There are no visible symptoms of this virus for years, and few young people have been tested for HIV. The best way to estimate is to look at the number of people between the ages of twenty and twenty-nine who have AIDS. In 1994, a total of 13,527 young adults in the United States were diagnosed with AIDS. Considering the number of years it takes for symptoms to appear, it is safe to assume that most of these people were infected with HIV when they were teenagers.

Given the number of people with AIDS who were infected with HIV during their adolescence, it is clear that this virus is a real threat to the millions of sexually active young people in the United States. Although anyone can contract HIV, even from only one risky incident, some young people are at greater risk for HIV infection than others because they engage in risky behavior more often.

SEXUALLY TRANSMITTED DISEASES (STDS)

One clear sign that millions of young people in the United States are having unprotected sex is the alarming rate at which teenagers are becoming infected with sexually transmitted diseases. Once known as venereal diseases (named after Venus, the goddess of love), STDs are infections and diseases passed from one person to another through sexual contact. Some, such as HIV and hepatitis, are also passed to others through the sharing of injection-drug needles and syringes. Experts estimate that a record number of Americans—more than 13 million people—contract an STD each year, half of whom are under the age of twenty-four. Interestingly, the number of different kinds of STDs is also at a record high. Before 1960, a venereal disease essentially meant gonorrhea or syphilis. Today, more than fifty types of sexually transmitted diseases are known.

If you are sexually active, you are at risk for contracting an STD. If you are sexually active and do not practice safer sex, you are at high risk for contracting an STD. Two of the most common, especially among teenagers and young adults, are bacterial infections called chlamydia and gonorrhea. Both can be cured with antibiotics, but if untreated, they can cause serious, long-term damage, including pelvic inflammatory disease in women and sterility in both men and women. Some symptoms, such as burning or pain while urinating and/or tenderness or inflammation of the genitals, may accompany these STDs. Most often there are no visible signs of infection.

AIDS

If you are sexually active, you are at risk for contracting an STD.

Two other very common STDs are genital warts and genital herpes, both of which are caused by viruses. Small bumps, blisters, or sores near the penis, vagina, rectum, or mouth are often, but not always, the primary symptoms of these viral infections. At least one million Americans are believed to be infected with genital warts and about 500,000 with genital herpes.

Although the symptoms of these infections can be treated, genital warts and herpes cannot be cured. Once infected, people will carry these viruses for life, experience periodic outbreaks of uncomfortable symptoms, and can pass them to sexual partners. These viruses also can cause serious damage to the reproductive system. Genital warts, for example, can cause cervical cancer in women and cancer of the penis in men.

Hepatitis, a dangerous virus that can cause severe damage to the liver, and syphilis, a bacterium that can cause blindness, brain damage, and death if untreated, are other sexually transmitted diseases now on the rise among teenagers and young adults.

Sexually transmitted diseases are highly contagious. They are easily spread to other people through unprotected sexual activity, and some, like genital herpes and warts, can be passed to infants during childbirth.

If they are not diagnosed and treated, STDs can cause serious and permanent damage to the genitals, the reproductive organs, the heart, the brain, and body joints.

STD infection is also linked to HIV infection. First, the presence of an STD indicates unsafe sexual behavior. If you have an STD, you have had or are having unprotected sex. The person who gave you this infection could also be infected with HIV. Second, if you have an STD, your immune system is waging a fight to rid the body of this infection and is less able to fight other germs, including HIV. Finally, and perhaps most important, the kinds of sores, blisters, and tenderness that accompany many STDs give HIV an easy pathway into the bloodstream.

Up to 80 percent of people who are infected with an STD do not have any symptoms of infection. In addition to being unaware of the damage the infection may be causing, asymptomatic people can pass the infection to others. Fortunately, some people experience symptoms that alert them to their condition. These may include:

For men:
Discharge from penis
Pain in testicles

For women:
Discharge and/or bad odor from vagina
Pain in pelvic area or lower abdomen
Pain in vagina during sex
Burning or itching in or outside vagina
Unusual bleeding from vagina

For men and women:
Swelling or tenderness of sex organs
Pain or burning during urination
Sores or blisters in or near sex organs,
    anus, or mouth

AIDS

> It is very difficult to talk to someone you don't know very well about practicing safer sex. You shouldn't be having sex with someone you don't know very well.

If you are sexually active, regardless of whether you have symptoms or not, you should have regular medical checkups to make sure you do not have a sexually transmitted disease. Most STDs can be completely cured with antibiotics, but it is essential that you take all of this medicine for the entire time it is prescribed. You should warn your past and present sexual partners that they may also be infected. Your partner should be tested and, if also infected, should receive and take his or her own medicine to treat the infection. Never share your medicine with other people. To protect yourself and others, you should refrain from having sex until your treatment is completed. If you do have sex, always use a latex condom to protect yourself and your partner.

SEXUAL ACTIVITY OF YOUNG TEENAGERS

In some communities in the United States, teenagers as young as thirteen and fourteen are already sexually active. Having only recently left middle school, very few of these young teenagers have developed the confidence and decision-making skills that a responsible and mature sexual relationship requires. Preventing pregnancy, STDs, and HIV infection requires good judgment, careful and consistent planning for protection, and an understanding of the consequences of behavior. In addition, the earlier that teenagers become sexually active, the more sexual encounters they will have before marriage or a long-term relationship. The more partners, the greater the chance that one of them may be infected with HIV or another STD. People who have unprotected sex with numerous partners are at high risk for HIV infection.

While a good number of happy, well-adjusted young people periodically engage in high-risk behavior, many others are struggling with serious economic, social, and emotional difficulties, including poverty, physical and sexual abuse, and neglect. Young adults who feel rejected or unloved by their families or unaccepted by their peers, come from troubled homes, are failing in school, or are dependent upon drugs often suffer from low self-esteem, depression, and loneliness. Many are desperate for acceptance and security. Too often, they think that sex will bring them the attention and love they seek.

GAY TEENS

Gay teens face many of the same developmental challenges as their straight counterparts: asserting their independence, discovering and accepting their identity, exploring their sexuality, and forming friendships and romantic attachments. Gay teenagers also face another hurdle during their adolescence: homophobia, the fear or hatred of homosexuals. Still widespread in our society, hostility toward gay people is especially acute during adolescence, where it is often marked by ridicule, cruelty, and even violence. It is no wonder, then, that many gay teens keep their sexual identity a secret during these years.

Jeff is a high school senior who has known that he is homosexual for several years, but has not told his friends or his parents.

Everyday I hear words like fag, sissy, queer, and much worse, in the halls of my school. Not to me, of course, because no one knows I'm "one of those people." I can't be myself here, not when I know how everyone, even my closest friends, think about gay people. Sometimes I even wonder if they're right, if there is something wrong with me, and then I feel terrible about myself. My only hope is that when I leave high school maybe I can just be myself and find other people like me, or at least people who will accept me.

The kind of isolation, rejection, and loneliness that Jeff describes is common among gay teenagers and young adults. Feelings of low self-worth, guilt, and shame are also common among gay teenagers. Jeff says that he has started to hang out in gay clubs to meet other people and admits to drinking and using cocaine during these times. Sometimes, he says, he does not practice safer sex. "It's hard enough just finding someone to go out with. I guess I don't always stop and think about safe sex, safer sex, condoms, AIDS, and all that."

Just like straight teens, gay teens are at risk for HIV infection if they engage in unprotected sex, have sex with numerous partners, use drugs and alcohol, or already have an STD. In addition, anal intercourse is a common sexual activity among gay men, and unprotected anal sex is a high-risk activity. Many organizations are devoted to helping gay teenagers stay safe and avoid infection with HIV. The organizations listed in Sources at the back of this book can assist you in finding help in your city or town.

STREET KIDS

Early sexual activity is common among street youth, teenagers who have left their homes or have been abandoned by their families. More than a million adolescents in this country spend each day and night in parks, in abandoned buildings, under bridges, in shelters, or on the streets of our cities. Everyday life for a homeless teenager is grim, dangerous, and often tedious.

Many use drugs and alcohol to deaden their pain and relieve the monotony of their lives. Living day to day entirely on their own, these teenagers are at the mercy of others for their most basic necessities. As a result, they often are taken advantage of by unscrupulous adults, as well as by other young people. Although they may be street smart, many fall victim to crime, abuse, sexual exploitation, drugs, malnutrition, and a myriad of diseases. Without financial or emotional support, some trade sex for money, shelter, food, or affection. Because survival sex rarely includes safe or safer sex, these young people have high rates of sexually transmitted diseases and are at very high risk for HIV infection.

AIDS is now the leading cause of death for Americans aged twenty-five to forty-four.

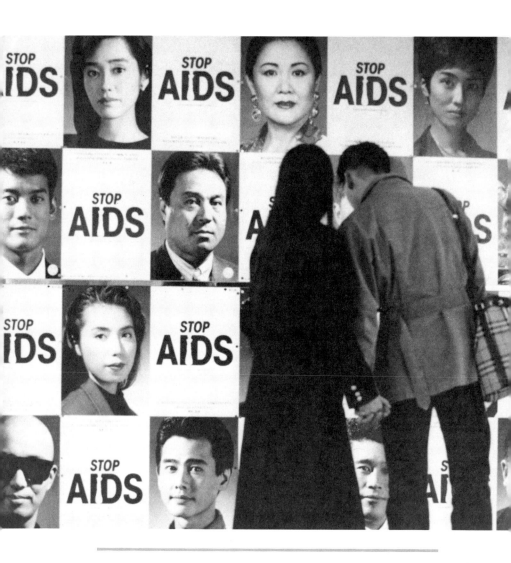

A young couple in a busy railway terminal in Tokyo pause to read posters for a "Stop AIDS" campaign. Japanese celebrities featured on the posters volunteered to participate in the campaign to educate young people about the disease and its prevention.

The risk of HIV infection is increased by either frequent, unprotected sex with numerous partners, drug and alcohol use, or the presence of STDs. Together, these factors spell disaster. Numerous agencies are devoted to helping teenagers at risk. If you or someone you know needs medical attention, drug treatment, counseling, or some other kind of assistance, be sure to call one of the helping agencies for teens listed in Sources at the back of this book.

TEENS WITH AIDS

Most young people who become infected with HIV during their teen years will not develop AIDS until their twenties. Some HIV-infected teenagers, however, already have AIDS-related diseases and infections. Of the reported 80,691 people diagnosed with AIDS in the United States in 1994, 417 were teenagers.[1] Although this number is expected to remain small compared with other age groups, it is increasing at an alarming rate. From 1989 to 1992, AIDS cases among people aged thirteen to twenty-four increased 77 percent, and some experts predict that the number of teens with AIDS will double every year.[2]

Many of the teens with AIDS in the United States today, about 30 percent of the total, contracted HIV from contaminated blood factors they took in the early 1980s to treat their hemophilia. Fortunately, testing of all blood and the heat treatment of blood products, which began in 1985, has nearly eliminated this kind of HIV transmission. By the end of the 1990s, we can expect very few young people to develop AIDS from transfusions and blood products. Although a minority contracted HIV from sharing needles, most adolescents with AIDS were infected through unprotected sex. Sexual contact, no doubt, will remain the principal way that teenagers and young adults will contract HIV in the years to come.

Teenagers with AIDS, like adults with AIDS, come from varied economic, ethnic, and racial backgrounds and from every state in the country. Some, like Krista Blake, one of several teenagers with AIDS featured in *Newsweek* in 1992, hardly fit the popular image of a person at high risk for HIV infection. When she found out she had AIDS, this "All-American" young woman was eighteen years old, on her way to college in Ohio, and discussing marriage with her boyfriend. She described her life as "basic, white bread America." She had only one risk factor, but it was a deadly one. At age sixteen she had unprotected sex with someone who was infected with HIV. She did not know he was infected at the time, but apparently he did know. "He knew that he was infected and he didn't tell me. And he didn't do anything to keep me from getting infected either."[3]

Many teenagers with AIDS and others at risk for HIV infection share Krista's background and experience. "Only" one risk factor is one too many, especially when that factor is unprotected sex.

Clinics and hospital programs throughout the country are providing specialized medical care, emotional support, and social services to the growing number of adolescents with AIDS and HIV infection. One such program is the Adolescent AIDS Clinic at the Montefiore Medical Center in New York City, where a team of health-care providers, social workers, and therapists work closely with about seventy HIV-infected teenagers. About half of these young people already have AIDS. It is very painful, says social worker Barbara Hershey, to witness such a debilitating and life-threatening disease among people so young. And, she explains, it is especially difficult for the kids themselves when someone in the group begins to lose a lot of weight, is suddenly hospitalized, or dies. These events, which happen frequently in this clinic, generally provoke strong reactions and difficult questions from the group: "Is this going to happen to me?" "How could she get so sick so fast?" "Does this mean I'm going to die"? "When am I going to die?"

It is important to note that this clinic is not filled only with grief, loss, and sickness. It also teems with love, support, and life. Despite the countless medical, family, school, and other social issues they must handle, these teenagers demonstrate great strength and hope. Several are young mothers struggling to provide a stable and loving home for their children. AIDS has even given some of these teenagers a sense of purpose they never experienced before. Now committed to helping other teenagers stay safe and avoid HIV infection, they devote their time to speaking at schools, leading workshops, and making educational videos. They hope that their efforts will help save the lives of the young people they reach.

HIV TESTING

If you have engaged in the kinds of unsafe behaviors discussed in this and other chapters, you are at risk for contracting HIV. It is never too late to change your behavior or to get help to stop taking chances with your life.

If you think you are at risk, or if you want to make sure that neither you nor your partner has been exposed to HIV, consider having an HIV antibody test. If you are not infected, you can finally put your worries aside and continue to protect yourself from HIV and other STDs. If you are infected, you can begin to get the medical treatment and emotional support you need. Chapter 6 describes what the HIV antibody test can tell you, how to go about finding the testing facility that is right for you, and what happens during the procedure.

6

HIV Testing

"I keep hearing about AIDS and I'm afraid maybe I have it and don't know it. I've never had sex, used needles, or had a blood transfusion."

"My boyfriend and I had sex for the first time last week. We didn't use any protection. Now I'm nervous that he gave me the virus."

"My boyfriend and I are gay. I know he had lots of relationships in the past. Should I be tested?"

"I shot drugs for a few years and used other people's needles. I have been clean for a year now. Could I be infected with HIV?"

All of these people are worried that they might be infected with HIV. They are not entirely at the same risk of having the virus, however.

- People who have never had sexual intercourse, never shared a needle, and never had a blood transfusion are at low risk for HIV infection.
- People who have engaged in unprotected sex or shared needles in the last ten years, or had a blood transfusion before 1985, are at risk.
- The number of sexual encounters and the kind of sex one has had can further increase risk.
- It could take only one risky incident to contract HIV.

The only way to know if you are or are not infected with HIV is to have a special kind of blood test. This is not a test for AIDS. It is a test that will tell you if you are infected with HIV, the virus that can cause AIDS. The test, however, cannot determine when you were infected, how much virus is present in your blood, or if or when you might develop AIDS.

THE ELISA AND WESTERN BLOT TESTS

The most commonly used HIV antibody test is the ELISA (enzyme-linked immunosorbent assay) test. First developed in 1985, ELISA is used to determine whether there is evidence of HIV infection in an individual's blood. This test also helps to ensure the safety of the nation's blood supply.

The ELISA test looks for HIV antibodies in a sample of blood, not virus particles themselves. Antibodies are the protein molecules that the immune system makes when foreign substances or antigens invade the body. In addition to alerting other immune-system cells of danger, antibodies neutralize many harmful microbes before too much damage is done to healthy cells. When HIV invades your body, your immune system responds by making special antibodies to fight the virus. Although they apparently are not always powerful enough to destroy HIV, these antibodies are present in your blood if you have been infected with this virus.

In general, a positive ELISA test result means that the test found HIV antibodies in the blood sample. This person was probably infected with HIV at some time. Those who test positive for the virus are said to be seropositive or HIV-positive (HIV+). A

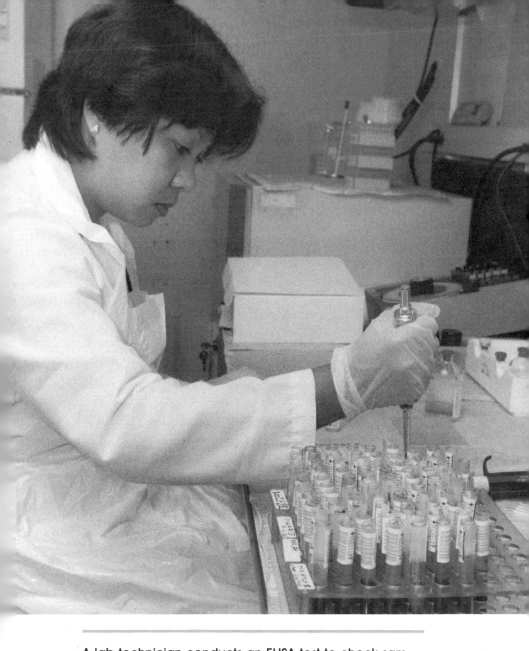

A lab technician conducts an ELISA test to check samples of blood for the antibodies that are present when an individual has been infected with HIV. Blood-donation centers across the country use this test to ensure that the blood used for transfusions is free of the virus.

negative test result means that HIV antibodies were not found in the blood sample. Because the results of an HIV test are so important, most laboratories will recheck any blood that shows evidence of HIV antibodies. If the second ELISA test detects HIV antibodies, the Western Blot test is conducted. An expensive and time-consuming procedure, the Western Blot is usually conducted only to confirm a positive ELISA test.

An antigen test, as the name implies, looks for particular antigens (viruses and other foreign substances that cause the immune system to produce antibodies) in blood samples. There are antigen tests that can find and measure the level of HIV in blood samples. At this time, HIV antigen tests are conducted primarily in research laboratories.

DECIDING TO GET TESTED

Joan decided to have an HIV test when she discovered that she had contracted genital herpes as a result of a single sexual encounter while on vacation.

I was in the mood to party that night, and I had too much to drink. I met someone who I thought was pretty special, and we ended up having sex. About six months later, I noticed these sores on my vagina. At first I was just embarrassed and angry about the infection, which I will have for the rest of my life. Then I realized that if he gave me this disease, he also could have given me HIV. I started worrying about it all the time. My friends told me not to worry, that you can't get HIV from only one time. But

I know that isn't true. Finally, I decided I needed to know for sure, and I made an appointment to get tested. I think deciding to have the test was much harder than actually going for the test. It really forced me to face the possibility that I actually might have the virus that causes AIDS.

Although HIV infection does not mean a person has AIDS, it is a serious, life-threatening condition. For many people the idea that they might have this virus is so terrifying that they are reluctant to get tested. Unfortunately, these are often the people who are at the greatest risk for infection. Some deny that it could happen to them; some downplay their risk factors; and some feel that they could not handle an HIV-positive result. Many are afraid that their parents, friends, or neighbors might find out about their test.

If you think you are at risk for HIV and are afraid to get tested for any of these or other reasons, you should speak with a doctor, health-care provider, school counselor, or a trusted, knowledgeable adult about your concerns. It's not a good idea to rely on the advice of your friends. As well-meaning as they might be, they may not know all the facts about your situation or about HIV infection in general. If there is no one you feel you can trust with your concerns, you can speak with an HIV/AIDS specialist on the phone. A trained counselor will answer your questions about your risk of infection and about HIV testing. You will not have to give the counselor your name, address, or age. The call is free and can be made at any hour of the day. You can find a list of state and national AIDS information hotlines in Sources at the back of this book.

WHERE TO GET TESTED

HIV-antibody tests are available at various sites throughout the country. You can arrange for a test through your doctor, who most likely will refer you to a hospital laboratory for the actual blood test. If you do not want to talk to your own doctor about this issue, or if you do not have a regular doctor, you can make your own arrangements. Community health centers, school-based health clinics, or public-health facilities frequently offer HIV testing. If you do not know what testing facilities exist in your city or town, you can call the National AIDS Hotline at 1–800–342-AIDS. A counselor can match your zip code with the testing center closest to you and can tell you what services it provides.

CHOOSING THE RIGHT TESTING CENTER

If you decide to get tested, you will want to know the clinic's rules and services so you can choose the right place for you. Call a few places and ask about their policies. At the very least, you should know if:

- there is a fee for the test
- pre-test and post-test counseling is provided
- a parent or guardian must accompany you
- anonymous testing is offered
- ongoing medical treatment is available

Although the HIV test is a simple procedure, it can be very stressful. Few people can anticipate how they will react to the experience. Choose a testing clinic that offers as much support as possible. Counseling before taking the HIV test and follow-up counseling to explain the results are essential.

PROTECTING YOUR PRIVACY

We all have had the painful experience of sharing a confidence with one person only to discover later that other people—classmates or acquaintances—"somehow" found out about your conversation. If you decide to have an HIV test, think carefully about whom you tell about your decision. This is a time when you need extra support and understanding. Only you know which people can give these to you and respect your privacy.

Your medical records are confidential. No one but you and your doctor or health-care provider should know about your health history or current condition.

HIV tests are also considered confidential and, therefore, no one but you and your doctor should know about your appointments, your conversations, or the outcome of your HIV test. Although doctors must respect your privacy, they also have a duty to warn people whose lives may be in danger. This means that, if another person's life is at stake, health-care workers may inform that person of your medical condition without your permission.

AIDS

A California jury found deceased actor Rock Hudson guilty of "outrageous conduct" for not disclosing his HIV infection to partner Marc Christian before his death from AIDS in 1985. Christian was initially awarded $21.7 million in damages.

It also is wise to remember that HIV test results may be recorded in your health records. Although usually these records are not shared with anyone else, they can be released if requested by a court or a health- or life-insurance company. In some states, doctors and clinics are required to report the names of people who test positive for HIV to their state public-health departments.

Because the possibility exists that HIV test results could be revealed to others, some people choose a clinic that offers anonymous testing. Here, you are not required to give your real name or any other personal information. Instead, you and your blood sample are given a matching number. No one knows or will know the results of the test but you.

COST

The charge for an HIV test ranges from $20 to $120. Medicaid and most private health-insurance policies cover the cost of HIV testing, and many clinics charge a sliding fee for the test based on your ability to pay. In addition, the Centers for Disease Control and Prevention (CDC) has established a number of free testing sites throughout the country.

GETTING TESTED

When you arrive at the center for your HIV test, you will meet with a counselor before your blood is taken. The counselor will explain everything you should know about HIV, AIDS, and HIV testing. It is normal to be nervous, to cry, and to feel helpless and afraid. Your counselor is not there to make judgments about you or your life, but to help you through this hard time and to answer all your questions.

Because your blood cannot be tested for HIV without your written permission, you will be asked to sign a consent form. In some states, people under a certain age need the permission of a parent or a guardian to get tested for HIV. The consent form not only gives the clinic permission to perform an HIV antibody test, but also states that you understand the test's purpose, its accuracy rate, and the meaning of both a positive and a negative result. You should fully understand these matters before you sign a consent form. If not, ask your counselor to go over anything that is not clear to you. If you need more time to think, make an appointment to come back at another time.

If you want to proceed, a nurse, doctor, or lab technician will take a blood sample. This person will wear rubber gloves as protection against getting nicked with the needle. Health workers take this precaution every time they draw blood, regardless of the reason for the test. The technician will clean the inside of your arm and insert a needle into your vein. Most people feel a pinch for a second when this is done. About a half ounce of blood is drawn into a syringe or container, which is then marked with your name (or a number).

This marked blood sample will be tested for HIV antibodies. This can take two to three weeks, depending upon how busy the lab is. When the test is completed, your doctor or counselor will call and ask you to come back to discuss the results. HIV blood tests can be confusing, so health workers want to explain the results to you in person.

A Negative HIV Antibody Test

A negative HIV antibody test result means that no HIV antibodies were found in your blood sample at this time. This most likely means that you are not infected with HIV. You should, however, repeat the test in another three months to be absolutely sure. Although most people develop enough HIV to be detected in blood within three weeks of infection, some people do not manufacture antibodies for months. During this time, which is called "the window period," a person could test negative for antibodies but still be infected. To make sure that your retest is accurate, it is very important that you do not engage in any risky behavior during this time. If your second test still shows that there are no HIV antibodies in your blood, you are not infected with the virus. This good news provides you with the opportunity to keep yourself safe and healthy.

I did a lot of crying and praying during the long two weeks I waited for that phone call. When the doctor told me my test was negative, I was never so relieved and happy in my whole life. I know that was the only time I could have been exposed to HIV and I know now that it will be the last.
—Joan, age 18

A Confirmed Positive HIV Antibody Test

A confirmed positive test result means that two separate ELISA tests and a Western Blot test found HIV antibodies in your blood. Although you may want to go through the testing process one more time to make sure that the tests were conducted properly, you should assume that you are infected with HIV.

AIDS

> "Wars and plagues have always been with us, but equally they always take us by surprise."
> Albert Camus
> *The Plague*

Many people who hear that they have tested positive for HIV are so shocked that they cannot believe it. Maria was only twenty years old when she learned that she had tested positive for HIV. Even though she knew she was at high risk because she had unprotected sex with someone who was already infected, she still had a hard time accepting the test results. "When I was told I was HIV-positive, I just sat and stared at the counselor. I insisted that there must be a mistake. This couldn't happen to me. I was so stunned that it was several days before the news even began to sink in."

The kind of shock that Maria describes is a normal reaction to very upsetting news. It is a response that protects us from feeling the full impact of a crisis all at once. Gradually, however, that numb feeling begins to wear off, and the long, sometimes painful, process of accepting a difficult and uncertain situation begins.

Who Should Know?

Although you should protect your privacy, certain people need to know if you are infected with HIV. First, you have an obligation to inform anyone whom you might have infected. If this is too hard for you to do yourself, many testing centers will notify people in your past or present life—without using your name—that they might be at risk for HIV.

Second, if you are a teenager, your parents should be told of your condition. Even if your relationship hasn't always been the best, chances are great that they love you. Besides caring deeply for you, they are also legally responsible for your medical treatment. Your counselor or doctor can help you figure out the best way to tell them and get them involved in your treatment.

LIVING WITH HIV INFECTION

Without a doubt, a confirmed positive HIV test is a very serious matter. If you receive the news that you are HIV-positive, it means that you are infected with the virus that causes AIDS.

It does not, however, mean that you have AIDS at this time, nor does it necessarily mean that you will get AIDS. Doctors cannot say with certainty why some people who are HIV-positive progress quickly to AIDS while others remain healthy for ten or more years after infection.

AIDS

"I heard this big thud, and then I found myself in the water. I just held my head in. . . . I didn't know if I was cut or not. But I wanted to hold the blood in, to just not let anybody touch it."

Olympic Gold Medalist Greg Louganis
New York Times, February 13, 1995

During those years, however, people infected with HIV or with AIDS are capable of infecting others, including sexual partners or anyone who uses needles they have used. If a woman who is infected becomes pregnant, she could transmit HIV to her unborn child. If you are infected with HIV, it is your responsibility to make sure that you do not transmit HIV to another person and that you keep yourself from being reinfected with HIV. You not only have a personal responsibilty to tell current and future partners of your medical status, but you are also bound by law to do so in many states.

Although no two individuals respond in exactly the same way, people who are diagnosed with an incurable, chronic infection like HIV often experience many of the same feelings about their situation. Disbelief or denial, terrible sadness, anger, anxiety, and guilt or shame are normal reactions. Sometimes these feelings come in stages; sometimes they seem to come all at once. A few people are overwhelmed by their situation and become very sick and depressed. Others feel that HIV has given them a unique opportunity to look at and experience life in a more positive way—with more purpose, inner peace, and hope.

HOPE FOR THE FUTURE

People living with HIV infection and AIDS need both emotional support and medical treatment to help them cope with and manage their conditions. At this time, there is no outright cure for HIV infection or AIDS. There are, however, many different treatments, therapies, and regimens that are helping people to survive this infection for many years.

7

HIV and AIDS Treatment

In August 1994, more than 10,000 people from around the world gathered in Yokohama, Japan, for the 10th International Conference on AIDS. The most renowned doctors, scientists, and public-health officials, as well as scores of AIDS activists and caregivers, presented the results of another year of AIDS research. They shared reports about the continued spread of AIDS, the devastating effect of the disease on families and communities, and the preliminary results of new types of drugs that aim to extend the health and life of HIV-infected people.

The scientists did not, however, announce the discovery of any "magic bullet" or miracle drug capable of curing or preventing HIV. Given the urgency of this international health crisis, this was a disappointment for the world, especially for the millions of people whose lives hang in the balance.

WHY ISN'T THERE A CURE FOR AIDS?

The fact that HIV challenges the best and brightest scientific minds in the world is not as remarkable as one might think.

- HIV is a virus. Like the common cold or the flu virus, it lives and reproduces inside healthy cells in the body. Doctors cannot kill a virus without damaging or destroying these very important cells. Therefore, germ-killing antibiotics, which are effective weapons against so many bacterial infections, such as strep throat or ear infections, cannot be used to fight viruses. Instead of medicines, we must depend on the body's natural system of defense—the immune system—to fight the viruses.

- HIV invades the most important disease-fighting cells in the immune system, which not only allows HIV to live and multiply in the body without much resistance but also destroys the body's ability to fight other infections. People do not die from HIV. They die from the opportunistic infections and diseases that flourish as a result of a damaged immune system.
- HIV is a retrovirus—a unique virus that reproduces differently from any other human virus. Scientists are still learning how HIV uses certain enzymes to "trick" healthy cells into giving the virus cells its genetic material so the virus can reproduce itself.
- HIV has a cunning ability to mutate or change. As a result of this tendency, thousands of different strains of the virus exist in the world. Because the virus can change its form within the body, one person can be infected with more than one strain of HIV.

All these factors make finding a cure for AIDS difficult. Although no one has given up hope that one day we will find a way to destroy the virus, much of today's research focuses on trying to stop or at least

slow the rate at which the virus invades and reproduces within our cells. Doctors hope that, even if
HIV remains a lifelong infection, they can find a way
to control the disease as they have with other chronic
illnesses such as asthma and diabetes.

Of equal urgency is preventing people from contracting the virus. In addition to educational programs
that stress safe behaviors, researchers are hopeful that
a vaccine to protect people from infection will soon
be available.

LIVING WITH HIV

*The words the counselor said were: "Your
test results came back positive," but the
words I heard were: "You are dying." And
for weeks after I learned that I was infected,
I felt and acted like my life was over. I
didn't eat. I didn't sleep. I hardly left my
house. I didn't speak to anyone. And then,
just as suddenly it seems, I decided to live.*
—John, age 25

Being infected with HIV, the virus that causes AIDS,
is not the same as having AIDS. It is, however, a
serious, chronic infection. "Deciding to live" takes
courage, hard work, and hope, and is the first of
many steps toward managing the infection. For John
and other HIV-positive people, this means taking excellent care of their physical and emotional health.
By paying close attention to basic health and nutrition, John can strengthen his immune system so it
can defend the body against infection, disease, and
the progression of HIV.

Although John had always paid attention to his health by working out in a gym and eating healthy food, he knew he had to do even more now that he was infected with HIV. The first step he took was to find a doctor who was experienced in treating people with HIV infection and with AIDS. John wanted to be sure that his doctor would have the most up-to-date information about the symptoms and treatments of this disease.

> I didn't want to go to my regular doctor, a guy who I know never saw anyone with AIDS. I was afraid he'd miss something important or wouldn't understand what I was going through. So I went to a clinic that specializes in sexually transmitted and infectious diseases and interviewed a couple of doctors and their nurse practitioners before I picked a team I felt comfortable with.

HEALTHY LIVING

One of the most important persons in John's life is his nurse practitioner, LuAnne.

> Of all the people in my life, she has given me the most support and the best advice. I've been HIV-positive and asymptomatic for three years. I don't think I would be this healthy if it weren't for her. She is always on my case about eating right, taking my vitamins, and getting enough sleep. And when I am really down—and there are plenty of down days—she's always there for me.

A kind, but no-nonsense caregiver, LuAnne makes sure that all her patients understand what they must do to stay healthy. Because certain substances and conditions (called cofactors) may speed up HIV production, she told John that it was essential that he eat nutritious meals, get plenty of rest, and exercise regularly and moderately. She also warned him that alcohol, recreational drugs, cigarettes, and excessive stress are cofactors he should avoid. These basic rules of healthy living, which most of us try to follow, are especially important for people infected with HIV because they help to keep the body's immune system strong.

REGULAR MEDICAL CHECKUPS

In addition to paying attention to nutrition and hygiene, John sees his doctor at the clinic every six months. Because early treatment of illnesses is so important, John's doctor examines and tests him for any signs of infections. His doctor also checks the level of T-cells in his body to measure the progress of the virus.

HIV-positive women need additional attention because they are at increased risk for sexually transmitted diseases, vaginal yeast infections, and serious cervical diseases and cancer. Doctors recommend that women infected with HIV have a complete gynecological exam, including a PAP smear, every six months. Because the virus can be passed to a child during pregnancy or childbirth, HIV-positive women should discuss pregnancy and birth control with their doctors. An HIV-positive woman who becomes pregnant needs special care and treatment for her own and her unborn child's health and safety.

> African-American and Hispanic women, who compose only 21 percent of the female population, account for about 77 percent of women with AIDS.
>
> from "Update: AIDS Among Women"
> *Morbidity and Mortality Weekly Report*
> February 10, 1995

CURRENT TREATMENT

Although there is still much we do not know about HIV and AIDS, our understanding of this virus and how it affects the body has increased tremendously since its discovery. Doctors, once bewildered by the unusual infections that affect people with AIDS, are now familiar with these illnesses and their symptoms and can quickly diagnose and treat them. In addition, scientists have developed several medicines that may help stop the virus from reproducing so rapidly. As a result of these and other advancements, people with HIV infection are staying healthy and living longer.

- Prophylactic or preventive medicines. These help to prevent or protect people from getting certain serious infections and illnesses, some life-threatening to a person whose immune system is damaged by HIV. Some also may speed up the virus and the onset of AIDS. People with HIV are particularly susceptible to various kinds of pneumonia, tuberculosis, herpes, and hepatitis. Antibiotics and vaccines can keep patients from contracting these diseases.

- Early detection and treatment of infections. Many of the infections and illnesses that affect people with AIDS can be treated and controlled if diagnosed early enough.
- Antiviral medicines. An antiviral medicine is one that slows the growth of a virus by interfering in some way with its ability to reproduce. Several drugs are available that aim to slow the growth of HIV, which in turn slows down the rate at which the virus invades the immune system and other cells in the body. The slower the virus reproduces within the body's cells, the longer the infected person stays healthy.

Azidothymidine (AZT), dideoxyinosine (ddI), dideoxycytidine (ddC), and stavudine (D4T) are the chief antiviral weapons used to control HIV infection. They work by blocking HIV's reverse transcriptase, an enzyme that the virus uses to invade and then reproduce in healthy cells. By disrupting this process, the drugs may slow down the pace of the virus. This, in turn, might allow the body to manufacture additional disease-fighting T-cells. The more T-cells the body has, the better equipped it is to fend off other diseases and infections.

Doctors usually recommend an antiviral medicine when an HIV-infected person's immune system begins to falter—when T-cells fall below a certain level or when an infection occurs that is known to be caused by a damaged immune system. Many people show dramatic improvement when they take these antiviral drugs—the level of virus in their blood often decreases, while that of their T-cells increases. At this time doctors are not sure if this change is actually related to the antiviral medication, to the ongoing battle between the immune system and the virus, or to other factors.

AZT and Mother-to-Infant Transmission

Although studies show that early treatment—before symptoms occur—with AZT may not be helpful, scientists have found that the drug can significantly reduce the transmission of HIV from an infected mother to her infant during pregnancy. One of the few "breakthroughs" in AIDS research, announced at the Yokohama conference, this finding is expected to prevent many children from contracting this deadly virus.

LIMITATIONS OF AZT

AZT and other antiviral medicines do not cure HIV infection or AIDS. In addition, experts disagree about whether such medicines affect the progress of the disease at all. These drugs also have many other serious drawbacks.

First, AZT is an expensive drug. It costs more than $2,000 per year per patient. In the United States and other industrialized countries, where the average income is high and access to health insurance and services is generally good, AZT is widely available and prescribed. Its high price, however, puts the drug out of reach for the millions of HIV-infected people in developing countries. These countries commonly are plagued by extreme poverty and the lack of adequate medical services and insurance. Ironically, these are the countries that are experiencing the worst of the AIDS epidemic.

Second, the effectiveness of AZT is frequently time-limited—the drug may stop working after a certain amount of time. Most doctors believe this is because HIV changes its structure, or mutates, rapidly. The drug that held the original virus in check then ceases to be effective against a new variety of HIV. To prevent this event, which is called viral resistance, doctors often recommend combination therapy—two or more antiviral drugs at the same time. The virus, however, continues its rapid mutations and often becomes resistant to all of the drugs.

Third, antiviral drugs such as AZT are so powerful that they can damage healthy cells and tissues in the body, causing serious side effects, including severe anemia, blinding headaches, and nausea.

ON THE HORIZON

In light of the many limitations of current antiviral medicines, researchers worldwide are investigating several new kinds of antiviral drugs. Early studies of a new class of drugs called protease inhibitors show promise. Like AZT, they aim to stop HIV from reproducing in healthy cells. While AZT blocks the enzyme reverse transcriptase, these drugs block protease, an enzyme that HIV uses to complete its reproduction. Doctors hope that these drugs will prove more effective than others in suppressing the virus. In addition, scientists hope that the discovery of the structure of the virus's third major enzyme, integrase, will open the door for the development of additional weapons against HIV. Although excited about increasing the number of available antiviral drugs, researchers are also cautious, warning that these new drugs may well suffer some of the same drawbacks as current treatments, including intolerable side effects and viral resistance.

Immune modulators are chemical substances that the body produces to help the immune system do its job efficiently. Interferon, as the name implies, "interferes" with viruses by attacking them when they are released from a cell and is also thought to attack certain cancerous tumors. This substance can be manufactured by scientists who are skilled in genetic engineering and is approved for the treatment of certain kinds of cancer. Doctors are testing interferon and several other immune modulators, including one called interleukin-2, to see if these substances can help people with AIDS and AIDS-related infections and cancers. Experiments with interleukin-2 show that the protein significantly increased the number of immune cells in some HIV-infected patients. "We think," explains Dr. Clifford Lane of the National Institute of Allergy and Infectious Diseases, "this is essentially the first time [anyone] has been able to therapeutically manipulate the immune sytem in a very substantial way."[1]

BONE MARROW TRANSPLANTS

In December 1995, doctors at San Francisco General Hospital performed an extraordinary but potentially fatal procedure when they injected millions of immune-system cells from the bone marrow of a baboon into the body of Jeff Getty, a 35-year-old man with AIDS. The baboon cells, selected because baboons appear to be resistant to HIV, will not cure Getty of AIDS; his own immune cells will remain infected.

Instead, doctors hope that the baboon cells will multiply in the patient's own bone marrow, providing him with additional, HIV-resistant immune-system cells. In theory, these healthy cells would prolong his life by helping him fight AIDS-related infections.

This procedure is expensive and risky. Baboon cell and organ transplants have been performed several times, but the patients' bodies rejected the foreign material. The possibility that Getty's body eventually will reject the cells is high. With his T-cell count at only one per microliter of blood, Getty was more than willing to take his chances.

To the surprise of many, including the doctors who warned that the operation might kill him, Getty survived this radical experiment and left the hospital feeling quite well. Doctors, however, are uncertain whether the baboon cells can function in Getty's body and help prolong his life. Even if this experiment is successful for this young man, cross-species transplants—animal to human—raise serious medical and ethical concerns, including the possibility of infecting a person with a dangerous animal disease. Doctors, who have seen the hantavirus, which rodents carry, cross over from animals to humans, are worried about the possibility of unleashing yet another deadly disease on the world.

VACCINE RESEARCH

The AIDS epidemic shows no sign of slowing its destructive path. Many countries in Africa have been devastated by the disease, and experts predict an even worse epidemic in Asia. In the United States the virus

Many celebrities have volunteered their talents to raise
funds so that scientists can continue research into treatments and vaccines for AIDS. In a concert at Madison
Square Garden to raise money for the Elizabeth Taylor
AIDS Foundation, the actress (second from right) was
joined by George Michael, Whoopi Goldberg, Lionel
Richie, and Elton John, among others.

continues to spread to new populations and areas of the country, especially among women, teens, and young adults. International health officials consider AIDS to be a global health emergency.

Modern medicine cannot kill HIV once it has infected the body. In fact, modern medicine cannot kill most viruses. It can, however, prevent people from getting numerous viruses. One way is to make sure that people are healthy and well nourished so that their immune system can fight disease. Aside from our own immune system, the vaccine is the most effective virus prevention we have. In light of the powerful strength of HIV and its continued spread worldwide, AIDS experts are planning to test two experimental AIDS vaccines. Dr. Peter Piot, chief of research at the World Health Organization's Global Program on AIDS, announced the decision in December 1994. The announcement was a surprise to some, coming just six months after U.S. AIDS specialists decided that the vaccines in question were not effective enough to proceed to the next phase of testing in this country.

Dr. Piot explained the WHO's decision to begin testing: "Representatives of developing countries stressed their tragic and dramatic plights and said they could not wait an eternity to test an HIV vaccine."[2] In other words, the infection rates are so high in some countries that a vaccine that might protect some people from infection is better than no vaccine at all.

The two vaccines under consideration are both derived from the gp 120 protein. Found on the surface of the virus, this protein helps HIV attach to human cells. Both vaccines have already completed two stages of testing. The third stage will involve from

3,000 to 20,000 volunteers. As in all scientific drug studies, some participants will receive the AIDS vaccine and some will receive a "dummy" vaccine, or placebo. This phase will last for several years, during which doctors will study and compare the rates of HIV infection among participants. Neither the researchers nor the volunteers will know which people received the real vaccine until the study is completed.

There is much work to be done before the vaccines can be tested. At this time, it is very likely that Brazil and Thailand, two countries that have asked to be considered, will be chosen as test sites. In addition to finalizing this decision, experts must also develop safe guidelines and educational programs so that volunteers understand the experiment. Because no one knows yet how effective the vaccines will be, all the volunteers must continue to protect themselves against HIV infection. Doctors must also decide how to measure the results of the testing. Although no vaccine is 100 percent effective, what rate of HIV infection will be acceptable?

"The world is really just one village. Our tolerance of disease in any place in the world is at our own peril."
Joshua Lederberg, President of Rockefeller University, in a speech to the Irvington Institute for Medical Research, Bankers Trust Company New York, February 8, 1994

HOLISTIC TREATMENTS

Holistic, or natural, medicine aims to control disease and relieve suffering by treating the whole person, not just the symptoms of illness. The health of the body, say holistic doctors, is directly related to the health of the mind and the spirit. Believing that the body has the power to heal itself, this approach uses natural substances and techniques to maintain or restore a healthy balance of the mind, spirit, and body. The most basic principles and techniques of this approach are already part of conventional medicine. We know, for instance, that proper rest, nutrition, exercise, and emotional well-being are powerful natural weapons against disease.

Numerous treatments fall into the broad category of "alternative" medicine. They include herbal extracts and mixtures, massage therapy, acupuncture, special diets, vitamin supplements, and meditation and relaxation. Used for thousands of years throughout Asia and other parts of the world, some of these therapies are gaining acceptance in this country as effective ways to prevent and treat modern ailments. Scores of doctors and HIV-infected people, faced with a dangerous disease and few effective treatment options, are turning to some of these therapies. They are using natural substances, vitamins, meditation, and spiritual energy to boost the immune system, relieve anxiety and depression, and control HIV infection. Several herbal compounds, widely available and used in China to fight viruses, are being tested by U.S. scientists as possible treatments for AIDS.

The medicines that fall into this category generally come from natural substances, but that does not mean that they are completely safe. Some herbal remedies, for instance, can be poisonous, and even vitamins, if too many are taken, can be dangerous. It is important to check with your doctor before experimenting with any medicine, natural or not, that you might have read about or heard about from others.

EMOTIONAL SUPPORT

It's not the same as having cancer. People still feel like it's your fault that you got AIDS. I didn't want to tell my parents I was HIV-positive because then I'd have to tell them how that happened. And I was as afraid of their reaction to the news that I was gay as I was of the news that I have AIDS.
—John, age 25

It is normal for people who are diagnosed with a serious or life-threatening illness to feel sadness, anxiety, fear, and loneliness. HIV-positive people often have additional worries because our society does not always treat them with acceptance, compassion, and understanding.

Many people with AIDS report being rejected by their families, dismissed from their jobs, and shunned by their communities. Some, fearful of such rejection, keep their medical condition a secret. As a result of bearing such worry and turmoil all alone, serious depression and even suicide are not uncommon among HIV-infected people and people with AIDS.

Even when friends and families are supportive and accepting, many HIV-positive people find that talking with others who are experiencing the same dif-

Film stars often wear a red ribbon when making public appearances, to show their support for AIDS awareness, as Tom Hanks did when accepting the Oscar for his performance in the film "Philadelphia," in which he portrayed a man infected with AIDS.

ficulties is helpful. Most communities have support groups where people with HIV and AIDS can meet regularly to talk about their feelings and share their experiences in a safe and nurturing environment. Support groups also are excellent sources of information about new medical treatments and various community services that others in the group may have found helpful to them.

Adolescence is generally a time of experimentation, self-discovery, and increased independence. Friends, school, dating, and social activities are very important during this time of life. They do not stop being important to teens who are HIV-positive. But these young people have other concerns as well: Can I continue in school? Whom should I tell? How can I help my parents cope? Will my boyfriend leave me? Can I still have sex? When will I get sick? Am I going to die? Both individual counseling and support groups especially for teens and young adults with HIV and AIDS are invaluable sources of comfort, support, and information. Many, like the AIDS Adolescent Clinic in New York, are linked to a hospital or a community clinic where medical treatment is also provided.

THE CHALLENGE AHEAD

Diseases, plagues, and global epidemics have existed throughout the human experience. Many have claimed far more lives than AIDS. History tells us that superstition, religious beliefs, and terror of infection often led to the isolation and abandonment of the sick. For the most part, past disease epidemics have been caused by germs that were highly contagious and struck their victims randomly.

HIV, as we know, is not an easy virus to get. It does not survive in the air, on our hands, or on objects. Instead, the spread of HIV depends almost completely upon human behavior. Human behavior, therefore, is the key to stopping the spread of AIDS. Societies in every country in the world are being challenged by this disease. How they respond to the challenge will determine the future role of AIDS in all our lives.

8

AIDS and Society: The Future

Since its sudden appearance in the United States in 1981, AIDS has claimed at least 4 million lives worldwide and more than 300,000 lives in the United States. Experts predict that by the year 2000 anywhere from 38 to 110 million people may be infected with HIV, the virus that causes AIDS. Although it is possible that not all of these people will develop AIDS, many millions will die from this disease in the next decade. Present in virtually every country in the world, this life-threatening virus is one of the most critical health issues facing nations today.

Of course, AIDS is not the first disease to cause so much suffering and loss of life in the world. Human history is filled with gruesome tales of devastating disease epidemics. In the fourteenth century, for instance, the bubonic plague claimed about 75 million lives in Europe, Asia, and Africa. This virulent bacterium, known as the Black Death, was responsible for wiping out at least a third of the world's population. A far more recent example, and one that some older Americans today may remember, is the influenza epidemic of 1918 that struck while World War I was being fought in Europe. This deadly flu virus killed nearly 22 million people worldwide in only one year.

Although the discovery of the cause of disease and the advent of antibiotics and vaccines during this century have significantly reduced the spread of and deaths from illnesses, they have not completely wiped out diseases or serious epidemics. On the contrary, a vast number of infectious diseases, both new and old, still threaten the modern world: Malaria kills about 4,000 people a day; measles will prove fatal to about one million children in the next year; and tuberculosis may take as many as 30 million lives by the end of the twenty-first century.

Many victims of modern diseases live in developing countries, where poverty, malnutrition, and inadequate medical care are widespread, and where such miracles of modern medicine as vaccines and antibiotics are scarce. But the link between poverty and poor health is also evident in the United States. In both inner cities and poor rural areas, millions of people are affected by extreme poverty, homelessness, drug use, overcrowded living conditions, and inadequate nutrition. These poor social conditions, medical experts agree, contribute to the presence and spread of many illnesses. The high rates of HIV infection and AIDS among poor, minority, and other disadvantaged people in our country confirm the urgent need to address various economic and social barriers to good health. To improve the health of all citizens, we must also improve educational and job opportunities, living conditions, and access to medical care and programs for drug-abuse prevention and treatment.

FEAR AND BLAME

Although AIDS is often called the plague of the modern world, it differs from past and present epidemics in several ways. Diseases like flu, malaria, and tuberculosis are caused by airborne germs. They are contagious—they can spread from one person to another quite easily, sometimes even through casual contact. HIV, on the other hand, is a sexually transmitted and blood-borne disease. Infection with this virus requires intimate contact with another person—principally through unprotected sex or sharing injection-drug equipment.

Although the number of people contracting HIV through heterosexual contact is on the rise, the majority—about 70 percent—of people with AIDS in the United States today are either homosexual men or injection-drug users. The fact that HIV infection is primarily caused by specific behaviors has had a profound impact upon the public's perceptions and opinions about people with AIDS. Some people in our society believe that people with AIDS, especially those they already view negatively, are personally responsible for their own condition and, therefore, do not deserve our sympathy and support.

No one "deserves" to get a deadly disease. People with AIDS, regardless of how they contracted HIV, need the same support and compassion as anyone else with a life-threatening condition. Few among us would consider shunning or blaming a relative who, after years of a sedentary life or a high-fat diet, suffers a debilitating stroke. Although we may be angry that our loved one didn't listen to medical advice, how many of us would actually blame or reject the person? How many of us would say, "What did he expect when he behaved that way?" We hope that sexually active people will heed public-health messages and practice safer sex. We hope that drug addicts will stop using drugs, stop sharing needles, and get the help they so desperately need. But if they do not, or cannot, should society turn its back on them?

AIDS AND PUBLIC SAFETY

Throughout human history, the fear of disease and death has affected the way people treat those who are sick or dying. It is said that epidemics bring out the very best and the very worst in societies—from heroic acts of compassion and self-sacrifice to heartless acts of cruelty and abandonment. When AIDS began spreading throughout our country, people were afraid that they might catch it. Even when assured by medical experts that HIV was not spread through casual contact, many were so fearful that they did not want children with AIDS to go to school with their children. They did not want people with AIDS to serve them food in restaurants, live in their apartments, or work in their businesses. A good number of health workers refused to treat or even touch people with AIDS. In 1992, when many basketball players did not want HIV-infected Magic Johnson to play on the court with them, he decided to retire from the sport he loved so much—even though he had not yet developed AIDS.

Today, because most people now understand that casual contact with HIV-infected people is safe, the kind of panic and fear exhibited during the early years of the epidemic is not so prevalent. For example, in 1996, Magic Johnson returned to the Los Angeles Lakers, and was welcomed back by fans and players.

State and federal laws help protect people from discrimination in most areas of everyday life in our country, including employment, housing, public education, medical treatment, and government-funded

In 1996, Los Angeles Lakers superstar Earvin "Magic" Johnson returned to the courts. Four years earlier, he had retired from the game when he learned that he was infected with HIV.

health insurance. Despite more than two hundred state and federal AIDS-related laws in effect, an ever-growing number of complex legal and ethical questions remain. One of the most important questions facing society is how to protect the health and safety of citizens without infringing upon the civil liberties of people infected with HIV. This issue is at the root of debates about social and medical policies.

Mandatory Testing

In the United States, HIV antibody tests are available to anyone who chooses to be tested. Only a few groups of people are required by law to take the test, including blood donors, military personnel, Peace Corps and Job Corps applicants and employees, federal prisoners, people seeking permanent immigration to our country, and, in some states, convicted prostitutes and sex offenders. If the majority of people infected with HIV are unaware of their infection and may be passing it to others, should we demand that more people, if not everyone, in the country be tested for HIV?

Supporters of mandatory testing believe that such a policy would protect the public from infection and help stop the spread of this virus. Even if only some of those who discover they are infected change their behavior, many lives could be saved. Routine screening for other diseases is already in effect. In order to get a marriage license, for example, couples must take a blood test to check for various STDs, and babies are routinely tested for STDs at birth. Many people suggest that similar large-scale testing for the presence of HIV be instituted as well.

AIDS

You can't get HIV from donating blood. A new, sterile needle is used each time that blood is taken.

Opponents of mandatory HIV screening would like to see doctors encourage people at risk, including pregnant women, to take the HIV antibody test, but strongly object to mandatory testing—both because such a policy could drive at-risk people away from health providers and would violate a person's right to privacy. Moreover, they argue, large-scale testing could increase the possibility of positive test results falling into the hands of government agencies, employers, health-insurance companies, or even, in the case of drug users, the police.

Some countries in the world restrict the activities of HIV-infected people, and many require large numbers of their citizens to be tested for HIV. Because our society places a very high value on personal freedom and civil liberties, mandatory HIV testing raises some very difficult questions:

Who would be targeted for testing?
Who would be in charge of deciding
     which groups to target for testing?
What agencies or people would have
     access to the test results?
Would mandatory testing lead to more
     isolation or perhaps even punish-
     ment of infected individuals?

The Right to Privacy vs. the Right to Know

While our society views an individual's civil rights, including the right to privacy and free speech, to be very important, it also holds that the general public has a right to be protected from harm or the threat of harm. We give every citizen in the country the right to speak freely, but we do not allow our citizens to infringe upon the rights and safety of the public at large. Yelling "Fire!" in a movie theater when there is no fire, as a famous example goes, is not allowed because it creates panic and endangers the lives of others.

Similarly, HIV-infected persons have the right to privacy about their medical status, but are not allowed to knowingly endanger the lives of other persons. To protect the rights of others, many states now require HIV-infected people to inform their partners of their medical status because not to do so would jeopardize lives.

In many states, people who know of their infection and continue to have sex without condoms or share needles with others can be arrested. If the courts prove that such behavior led to another person's infection with HIV, the accused person can be charged with attempted murder or assault with intent to kill. If the behavior led to another person's death, the accused could be charged with manslaughter. There already have been several criminal and civil AIDS-related cases successfully tried in our courts, and many more can be expected in the future. Although these laws may deter some people from intentionally harming others or acting irresponsibly, they do not address the most common way this virus is spread—unknowingly.

HIV-Infected Doctors and Patients

Because HIV can spread to others through contact with blood and other body fluids, both patients and health-care workers are at potential risk for infection—from each other. At this time, neither doctor nor patient is obliged to inform the other if he or she is infected with HIV. For instance, about 7,000 doctors are infected with the AIDS virus. Should they be required to inform their patients of their status, even if the procedures they perform pose no risk to others? If so, how many people would allow an HIV-infected doctor to treat them? Similarly, should patients be required to inform their doctors or dentists that they are infected? Hospitals now routinely test patients for hepatitis and tuberculosis upon admission so they will not spread these diseases to others. Many people think that doctors, especially surgeons, also have a right to know if their patients are infected with HIV. Opponents, however, say that the universal precautions recommended by the Centers for Disease Control and Prevention (CDC), and described in Chapter 3, sufficiently protect medical workers and other professionals from contracting or transmitting HIV.

AIDS

In a 1991 poll, 90 percent of the people said that all health workers should be required to tell patients if they are infected with HIV; 97 percent said that HIV-infected patients should be required to tell health workers.

Newsweek
July 1, 1991

HIV-infected Athletes

In 1988 the American athlete Greg Louganis won the gold medal for diving at the Summer Olympics in Seoul, South Korea. During a qualifying dive, Louganis, who had also placed first in the 1984 Olympics, hit his head on the diving board, which caused a large cut that required stitches. In February 1994, Louganis announced that he had AIDS. He also revealed that he knew he was infected with HIV during the 1988 Olympics. Except for Louganis, his personal physician, and his coach, no one knew about his condition, including the doctor who stitched the cut on his head. This doctor, who has since tested negative for HIV, was not wearing latex gloves when he stitched the diver's cut. It is not known whether Louganis spilled blood on the diving board or in the pool, but the chance of another person's contracting virus from blood in a chlorinated pool is extremely remote, if not zero. Even so, the Louganis incident reopened public debate about HIV and sports-related injuries. Should athletes be tested for HIV? If infected, should they be allowed to compete? If infected, do they have an obligation to inform their teammates, opposing players, coaches, or medical authorities?

Athletes, especially those who play contact sports like football and hockey, often receive injuries that cause bleeding. Authorities believe that the risk to other players, should an injured player be infected with HIV, is small. In fact, a National Football League study puts the risk at about one in a million.[1] Given this low risk, and the lack of a single case of HIV infection from one athlete to another through a bleeding incident, U.S. professional and amateur athletes are not required to take an HIV antibody test or reveal their status to others. Instead, sports officials require that any player who has a bleeding injury be removed immediately from the game. Doctors who treat injured athletes now wear rubber gloves and practice universal precautions to protect themselves from possible infection.

Immigration and Travel

HIV infection and AIDS now exist in nearly every country in the world. Fear of this virus and concern for the health of their citizens have prompted at least forty-two nations to require HIV antibody tests of some foreign visitors. The United States, for instance, does not allow entry to HIV-infected people seeking permanent immigration to our country. Other nations are more restrictive. Russian authorities are considering a proposal to require HIV antibody tests of all visitors to that country. AIDS activists and other concerned world leaders think that restricting international travel of HIV-infected people is a form of discrimination and is not an effective way to slow the spread of this epidemic. "It would be an illusion to think that certain countries can protect themselves alone by closing their border," warns Prime Minister Edouard Balladur of France.[2]

Those who favor travel restrictions point out that the United States already forbids visitors with syphilis, gonorrhea, leprosy, and tuberculosis from entering the country, so why should those infected with a virus that can cause a deadly disease be judged differently? Opponents argue that HIV does not pose the same kind of threat to our citizens as contagious diseases like tuberculosis. President Bill Clinton has proposed changing our immigration laws. He suggests that people with infectious diseases, and active tuberculosis in particular, should be forbidden entry to the United States, while those with sexually transmitted and blood-borne diseases, which are not transmitted through casual contact, be allowed to travel freely. This idea, which has strong support among public-health officials, will be the subject of lively debate in Congress.

EDUCATION AND PREVENTION

Gay men were the first group of Americans to contract HIV and develop AIDS in the United States, and they composed the majority of AIDS cases in the United States for the first decade of this epidemic. As sickness and death spread quickly, the gay community sprang into action, educating themselves and the country about AIDS and HIV transmission and prevention. Posters, pamphlets, free condoms, educational workshops, and informational hotlines provided information and preventive advice to thousands of at-risk people. As a result of these intensive efforts, gay men quickly began reducing their risks by practicing safer sex and limiting the number of sexual partners. There is no question that these strategies paid off. In 1986 more than 70 percent of AIDS cases were among gay men. Today, gay men account for about 43 percent of newly diagnosed AIDS cases. Clearly, AIDS education can change personal behavior and prevent the spread of AIDS. Experts warn, however, that the battle is far from over for this group of people. Gay men need to maintain the safe behaviors they've adopted, and young gay men—teens and college students—must adopt these behaviors as soon as they become sexually active.

As a result of the lessons learned from the first AIDS activists, AIDS education and prevention are now taught in public schools in the United States, usually as early as middle school. Public-health announcements that advise the use of condoms are aired at night on television stations. Social workers and public-health workers in large cities distribute pamphlets, needle sterilization kits, and condoms to people at high risk for HIV infection. These activities are aimed to stop the spread of HIV, but they are not popular with everyone in our country.

AIDS EDUCATION IN PUBLIC SCHOOL

Parents, teachers, and public-health workers generally agree that young people need to know what HIV is and how they can avoid exposure to this virus. They do not, however, always agree about what information and advice should be given to students. Some parents think that detailed discussions about sexuality, birth control, homosexuality, and safer-sex practices will help their children make good choices and stay safe, while others believe that they encourage young people to become sexually active. Parents who believe that premarital sex and/or homosexuality are immoral are at odds with school courses that do not stress abstinence or do not present their moral and religious ideas. And they are at odds with suggestions that students might obtain condoms from their school health clinics—even though schools with such programs already require parents to sign a permission form before allowing a student to participate.

Similar debates are also taking place in local and state governments, where legislators and public-health officials are battling a variety of issues, including the

Education plays an essential role in preventing the spread of AIDS. Tyler Nash, age seven, and his brother Bran, age twelve, have accessed computer information on the subject at San Francisco's Exploratorium.

language and message of public-health pamphlets, condom and bleach-kit (for sterilizing needles) distribution programs, and clean-needle exchange programs. Some citizens oppose these efforts on the grounds that they encourage immoral and criminal behavior. Public-health workers and most AIDS activists, however, believe that it is impossible to stop the spread of AIDS without discussing sex in a frank manner or providing the tools—condoms and clean needles—to prevent the transmission of HIV. Approximately one million people in our country are infected with HIV. Most of these people will likely develop AIDS. If we want to prevent such a prospect for the future, what steps are we willing to take?

HOPE FOR THE FUTURE

After years of exhaustive studies by thousands of researchers, the human immunodeficiency virus continues to challenge the most renowned medical experts in the world. There is no question, however, that we have learned an astonishing amount about this virus and the diseases that result from its attack on the immune system. Not only have we isolated the cause of AIDS and developed a reliable test for HIV antibodies, but we also have developed a treatment that dramatically reduces the chances of an infant's contracting the virus from an infected mother. The early diagnosis of opportunistic infections and drug therapy to treat them can now prolong and improve the quality of life for people with AIDS. It is unfortunate that the extraordinary scientific achievements that have taken place in such a short time are so often overlooked because they have not yet led to a cure for this unique virus.

AIDS

> "The global AIDS problem speaks eloquently of the need for communication, for sharing of information, and experience, and for mutual support; AIDS shows us once again that silence, exclusion, and isolation—of individuals, groups, or nations—creates a danger for us all."
>
> Jonathan Mann, January 1988
> World Summit of Ministers of Health on
> Programmes for AIDS Prevention, London

Intensive research continues, and no one has given up hope that someday we will find a way to rid the body of this elusive virus once infection has occurred. To this end, scientists are continually uncovering new information about how HIV invades and destroys cells.

In the fall of 1995, doctors in Australia reported that a group of HIV-infected people, who show no signs of immune damage after fourteen years, are infected with a strain of HIV that is missing an essential component—the nef gene. Without the nef gene, HIV apparently loses its ability to infect and damage healthy cells.

In the December 1995 issue of *Science*, Dr. Robert Gallo, director of the Institute of Virology at the University of Maryland, reported the results of his work with HIV and immune-system chemicals called chemokines. His laboratory tests showed that three chemokines, which are released by CD 8 cells when a foreign substance is present, stopped HIV from growing. During the same month, Dr. Reinhald

Kurth, president of the Paul Erlich Institute in Germany, revealed that interleukin 16, a hormone produced by CD 8 cells, stopped HIV from replicating in African green monkeys. Because humans manufacture a nearly identical hormone, it is possible that our natural defense system also stops HIV from growing after it has infected the body.

Doctors also continue to test new weapons, including antiviral drugs, gene therapy, and immune boosters to delay the progression of HIV infection, as well as others to treat debilitating and fatal opportunistic infections. In the fall of 1995, for instance, doctors announced the availability of a drug-implant procedure to treat cytomegalovirus retina, which affects about 40 percent of people with AIDS and often causes blindness. This new procedure is expected to help save the eyesight of thousands of people with this disabling infection.

All these findings have excited AIDS experts all over the world, who hope that they will speed vaccine development, expand treatment options, and improve the quality of life for people with AIDS. Should a vaccine prove effective in preventing infection with HIV, the world will have found the miracle it has been awaiting.

Despite their numerous achievements in AIDS research and treatment, however, scientists have yet to unlock all the mysteries of this virus. In fact, it is possible that medical science will not defeat HIV in our lifetime—if ever. This discouraging possibility does not mean that HIV infection has to remain the scourge it is today.

Although the world has yet to abandon hope for a medical miracle—a "magic bullet"—to cure this disease, most experts believe that preventing infec-

Today, almost one million Americans are infected with HIV. How's it all going to end?

One in 250 Americans is infected with HIV.

1-800-342-AIDS

AMERICA RESPONDS TO AIDS

U.S. DEPARTMENT OF HEALTH & HUMAN SERVICES   CDC
Public Health Service

tion, rather than curing infection, is the surest way to rid the world of this modern plague. The AIDS epidemic is being fought not only in high-tech laboratories but also on city streets, in school classrooms, and in health-care centers. Here, as well as in other arenas, AIDS education and prevention messages are reaching millions of people at risk for HIV infection. Committed and hardworking educators, social workers, and teenagers like yourself are already having an impact on the lives of young people at risk for HIV infection. Because HIV is not spread through casual contact, we can protect ourselves from ever being exposed to this virus and never have to worry about getting AIDS.

The war against AIDS ultimately may be won—and can be won—by permanently changing sexual attitudes and behavior and by confronting another plague of the modern world: drug abuse. These are not easy tasks, but as we face yet another decade of suffering and loss among the world's families, they must be undertaken immediately. At the Global AIDS Summit in Paris in 1994, countries from around the world came together to pledge their commitment to stopping the ongoing AIDS epidemic. The rich and poor nations, participants pledged, must work together to stop the spread of AIDS by sharing scientific knowledge, medical resources, and money for research, education, and treatment. South Africa's leader Nelson Mandela's stirring words at this meeting attest to the urgency of the work ahead of us and to an ever-growing spirit of global cooperation: "AIDS knows no custom. It knows no color. It knows no boundaries. We have to work together wherever we are to preserve our nation, our continent and humanity as a whole." [3]

Notes

CHAPTER 1
1. Remer Tyson, "AIDS Hangs Over Young Kenyans' Future," *Detroit Free Press*, September 30, 1995. Located in CD NewsBank (Compact Disc), NewsBank, Inc.
2. *Facts on File*, August 18, 1994, p. 579.

CHAPTER 3
1. Gerald J. Stine, *AIDS Update: 1994–1995* (Englewood Cliffs, NJ: Prentice-Hall, 1995), p. 110.
2. *Facts on File*, June 30, 1994, p. 463.
3. Stine, p. 172.
4. Earvin (Magic) Johnson, *What You Can Do to Avoid AIDS* (New York: Times Books, 1992), p. 4.

CHAPTER 5
1. Morbidity and Mortality Weekly Report, "Update: Acquired Immunodeficiency Syndrome—United States, 1994," Vol. 44/No.4, February 3, 1995, p. 65.
2. Stine, p. 206.
3. Lucille Beachy, "Teenagers with AIDS," *Newsweek*, August 3, 1992, p. 49.

CHAPTER 7
1. Doug Levy, "Treatment Helps Repair HIV Damage," *USA Today*, March 2, 1995, p. 1A.
2. Lawrence K. Altman, M.D., "After Setback, First Large AIDS Vaccine Trials Are Planned," *The New York Times*, November 29, 1994, p. C3.

CHAPTER 8
1. Jere Longman, "Doctor at Games Supports Louganis," *The New York Times*, February 13, 1995, p. B15.
2. Alan Riding, "Paris Meeting Backs U.N. Program to Combat AIDS, *The New York Times*, December 1, 1994, p. A12.
3. "42 Nations Attend AIDS Summit," Associated Press News Service, November 30, 1994. Located in CD NewsBank (Compact Disc), NewsBank, Inc.

Glossary

Abstinence: the act of refraining from an activity. Sexual abstinence means refraining from having sex.

AIDS (Acquired Immune Deficiency Syndrome): a group of illnesses that result when a virus called HIV attacks and destroys immune-system cells.

Alternative medicine: treatments, medicines, and techniques that rely on natural substances and methods to relieve suffering and disease; includes herbs, massage, acupuncture, and meditation.

Anal intercourse: a sexual act in which a male inserts his penis in the rectum of his partner.

Antibody: a protein produced by B-cells that protects against disease.

Antigen: a foreign substance that causes a reaction from the immune system, such as the production of antibodies or an increase in white blood cells.

Antigen test: a test that looks for specific diseases.

Antiviral drug: a medicine that stops or controls a virus.

Asymptomatic: infected with a disease but showing no symptoms.

AZT (azidothymidine): an antiviral drug used to treat HIV infection. Aims to prevent HIV from multiplying in healthy cells by blocking the enzyme reverse transcriptase.

Bacteria: one-celled organisms; some are beneficial and some cause disease.

B-cells: white blood cells that produce antibodies to create immunity against disease.

Bisexual: a person who has sex with both males and females.

Body fluids: any liquids found in the body. Include blood, urine, tears, semen, and vaginal secretions. HIV can be passed on to another person through the exchange of blood, semen, and vaginal secretions.

Bone marrow: the soft tissue that fills the cavities of the bones; the source of all blood cells.

Cancer: a group of diseases characterized by uncontrolled growth of and spread of abnormal cells.

Candidiasis: an infection of the mucous membranes of the mouth, esophagus, and vagina caused by a fungus. Also called *thrush*.

Casual contact: everyday physical contact with another person. Touching, hugging, most kinds of kissing, and sharing the same air, drinks, food, and toilet are examples of casual contact. HIV is not transmitted through casual contact.

CD4 protein: the cell receptor for HIV; a surface protein found on T-cells, macrophage cells, and some cells in the brain and other organs. Cells with this protein are often called CD4 cells.

Cell: unit of living matter in bodily organs or within the bloodstream.

Cell-mediated immunity: immunity provided by the T-cells.

Chlamydia: a common sexually transmitted disease caused by a bacterium.

Cofactors: elements that can affect the progression of a disease or increase the likelihood of developing a disease. Drug use, malnutrition, tuberculosis infection, and sexually transmitted diseases are thought to be cofactors of HIV infection and AIDS.

Condom: a thin, protective sheath for the penis used to prevent STDs or pregnancy.

Cytomegalovirus (CMV): a herpes virus that commonly affects HIV-infected people. May cause pneumonia. Cytomegalovirus retina infects the eye, often causing blindness.

Dementia: loss of mental abilities, including memory, reasoning, concentration, and judgment. Many people in advanced stages of AIDS suffer from this condition.

Disease: a disorder with a specific cause and characteristic symptoms.

DNA (deoxyribonucleic acid): a complex molecule that carries genetic information.

ELISA: blood test to find antibodies to an antigen. The HIV ELISA test indicates if antibodies to HIV are present, which means HIV is in the bloodstream.

Enzyme: a substance produced by living cells that creates chemical reactions.

Epidemic: an outbreak of a disease that surpasses the expected rate in a particular geographical area.

Gay: colloquial term for a person who is homosexual.

Hemophilia: a hereditary disease in which the blood does not clot as well as it should. Caused by a lack of certain blood-clotting factors in the blood.

Herpes simplex: a group of viruses that cause painful blisters or sores in the mouth or genital area. The most common sexually transmitted disease.

Herpes varicella zoster virus (HVZ): the virus that causes chicken pox in children. In adults, the herpes zoster virus, also called shingles, causes painful blisters on the skin along nerve pathways. Common among people with AIDS, this virus can cause infection throughout the body.

Heterosexual: a person who has sex with someone of the opposite sex.

HIV (Human Immunodeficiency Virus): a retrovirus that most doctors believe causes AIDS. Previously called HTLV-III, LAV, and ARV. Most common form, found in North America, Europe, Asia, and Africa, is called HIV-1.

HIV-2: a retrovirus similar to HIV-1 found primarily in western Africa.

HIV positive: refers to the presence of HIV antibodies, which indicates the presence of HIV in the body.

Homophobia: fear or negative opinion of homosexuals.

Homosexual: a person who has sex with someone of the same sex.

Humoral immunity: protection against disease that antibodies provide.

Immune boosters or **modulators:** substances that improve the functioning of the immune system. Interferon and interleukin-2 are immune modulators.

Immune system: cells and proteins that protect the body from diseases and infections.

Immunity: the condition of being protected against or resistant to a disease. May be provided by the body's own immune system or by vaccine.

Immunodeficiency: a state in which the immune sytem is not working properly. Can be the result of malnutrition, cancer-fighting drugs, or certain diseases like HIV.

Incubation period: the time between infection with a microorganism and the onset of symptoms of disease.

Infection: the contamination of an organism with a disease.

Injection drug use (IDU): the use of drugs that are delivered into the vein or muscle with a needle. One common way HIV is transmitted.

Kaposi's sarcoma: a rare form of cancer of the connective tissue, usually involving the skin, that commonly affects people with AIDS.

Lymphadenopathy: persistently enlarged lymph nodes or swollen glands, often accompanied by fever and weight loss. May indicate early stages of active HIV infection.

Lymph nodes: small collection of tissues that contain large numbers of lymphocytes. The lymph nodes filter out foreign particles and cells.

Lymphocyte: a type of white blood cell responsible for immunity. T-cells and B-cells are lymphocytes.

Mandatory testing: disease testing that is required. Certain government jobs require applicants to be tested for HIV.

Monogamous: describes a relationship, usually involving sex, with only one person.

Opportunistic infection: an infection caused by a common, usually harmless germ that causes serious disease in people with damaged immune systems.

Parasite: a plant or animal that lives on or in another organism; usually causes harm.

Phagocyte: a type of white blood cell responsible for immunity. Macrophages and granulocytes are phagocytes.

Pneumocystis carinii pneumonia (PCP): a lung infection caused by a protozoan parasite that can cause pneumonia; a common opportunistic infection of people with AIDS.

Protease: an enzyme that HIV uses to complete its replication.

Retrovirus: a virus that contains RNA as its genetic material; HIV is a retrovirus.

Reverse transcriptase: an enzyme that HIV uses to convert its RNA to DNA so it can multiply.

RNA (ribonucleic acid): a complex molecule similar to DNA.

Semen: the fluid that is ejaculated from the penis when a male has an orgasm.

Seroconversion: the change in an HIV-antibody blood test from negative to positive; occurs when HIV antibodies are produced and detected in the blood after infection. See also *Window period.*

Sexual intercourse: the sexual act in which a male inserts his penis inside another person's vagina or rectum.

Sexually active: engaging in vaginal, oral, or anal sex.

Sexually transmitted disease (STD): one of about fifty diseases that are spread through sexual contact. Chlamydia, genital herpes, genital warts, and gonorrhea are common STDs. HIV is also a sexually transmitted disease.

Syndrome: a group of symptoms occurring together that characterize a specific disease or condition.

T-cell: a lymphocyte that matures in the thymus and is responsible, both directly and indirectly, for protecting the body against infections.

T-helper cell: a type of T-cell that regulates the immune system's response to infection by alerting other cells to the presence of a pathogen and by assisting the B-cells in producing antibodies.

T-killer cell: a type of T-cell that directly attacks germs and foreign particles in the body.

T-suppressor cell: the T-cell that stops the production of antibodies; calls off the immune system's response to an antigen.

Tuberculosis: a serious bacterial infection, most often settling in the lungs. Often a cofactor or an opportunistic infection of HIV.

Unprotected sex: oral, vaginal, or anal sex that occurs without the use of a condom or dental dam.

Vaccination: a preparation of killed or weakened microorganisms introduced into the body to produce immunity to a specific disease by causing the body to produce antibodies.

Vaginal secretions: fluids found inside the vagina.

Viral replication: the process that a virus uses to produce more viruses.

Virus: a microorganism composed of genetic material, either RNA or DNA and protein, that lives and multiplies within living cells in the body.

Wasting: a syndrome characterized by severe weight loss, weakness, night sweats, diarrhea, and fever that commonly affects people in advanced stages of AIDS; these symptoms can be caused by a bacterial infection called mycobacterium avium intracellulare (MAI) or by mycobacterium tuberculosis (TB).

Western Blot test: a test used to detect HIV antibodies in the blood, usually administered to confirm a positive ELISA test.

Window period: the time between HIV infection and the production of antibodies. This period ranges from a few weeks to six months or perhaps even longer. Before HIV antibodies are produced, an HIV antibody test will be negative; after antibodies are produced, the blood test will be positive.

Sources

FOR INFORMATION:

The American Red Cross
National Aids Education Office
1730 D Street, N.W.
Washington, D.C. 20006
Phone: 202-737-8300
Supplies materials for the purpose of AIDS education and prevention to individuals, community groups, and teachers.

CDC National AIDS Clearinghouse
1-800-458-5231
Hours: 9 a.m. to 7 p.m., Monday to Friday
Provides information about clinical drug trials, referrals for testing and treatments, and current HIV/AIDS research materials.

CDC National AIDS Hotline
1-800-342-2437 (English)
1-800-344-7432 (Spanish)
1-800-243-7889 (Hearing Impaired)
Hours: Twenty-four hours a day, seven days a week. Provides general HIV/AIDS information, as well as referrals for HIV state testing sites, treatment, counseling, and drug and alcohol treatment.

Gay Men's Health Crisis
1-212-807-6655 (New York)
Provides support, counseling, and referrals for services; sensitive to the concerns of gay men and teens.

HEAL (Health Education AIDS Liaison)
1-800-410-4325
Provides information about natural and alternative medicines and treatments.

National Clearinghouse for Alcohol
and Drug Information
1-800-729-6686
Hours: 8 a.m. to 8 p.m.
Provides referrals for substance abuse treatment and information, publications, and statistics about substance abuse and AIDS.

National Native American AIDS Hotline
1-800-283-2437
Provides information about HIV/AIDS, geared to Native American people.

National Runaway Switchboard
1-800-621-4000
Hours: Twenty-four hours a day, seven days a week.
Provides information about available services to runaway teens.

National Sexually Transmitted Diseases Hotline
American Social Health Association
1-800-227-8922
Hours: 8:00 a.m. to 11:00 p.m., weekdays.
Provides information about STDs.

People with AIDS Coalition Hotline
1-800-828-8380
Hours: 8 a.m. to 5 p.m., Monday through Friday
Provides Information about current AIDS treatment options and support services.

Project Inform
1-800-822-7422
Hours: 10:00 a.m. to 4:00 p.m. (Pacific Time) weekdays and 10:00 a.m. to 2:00 p.m. Saturdays.
Provides information about current HIV and AIDS
treatment, especially alternative medicines.

Teenagers' AIDS Hotline
T.A.P. (Teens Teaching AIDS Prevention)
303 Walnut Street
Kansas City, MO 64101
Phone: 1-800-34-TEEN
Hours: 4:00 p.m. to 8:00 p.m.
A hotline for teenagers, run by teenagers. Trained
staff provides information about HIV, AIDS infec-
tion, testing, treatment, and prevention.

Youth Crisis Hotline
1-800-448-4663
Hours: Twenty-four hours a day, seven days a week.
Christian organization that offers intervention, information, and referrals to teens in crisis.

STATE HOTLINES:

(Those marked with * provide information especially
for teens)

Alabama	1-800-228-0469
Alaska	1-800-478-2437
*Arizona	1-800-334-1549
Arkansas	1-800-448-8305
California	
Northern	1-800-367-2437
Southern	1-800-922-2437

Colorado	1-800-252-2437
*Connecticut	1-203-566-1157
Delaware	1-800-422-0429
District of Columbia	1-202-332-2437
Florida	1-800-352-2437
Georgia	1-800-551-2728
Hawaii	1-800-922-1313
Idaho	1-208-345-2277
Illinois	1-800-243-2437
Indiana	1-800-848-2437
Iowa	1-800-445-2437
Kansas	1-800-232-0040
Kentucky	1-800-654-2437
Louisiana	1-800-922-4379
Maine	1-800-851-2473
Maryland	1-800-638-6252
Massachusetts	1-800-235-2331
Michigan	1-800-872-2437
Minnesota	1-800-248-2437
Mississippi	1-800-537-0851
Missouri	1-800-533-2437
Montana	1-800-233-6668
Nebraska	1-800-782-2437
Nevada	1-800-842-2437
New Hampshire	1-800-872-8909
New Jersey	1-800-624-2377
New Mexico	1-800-545-2437
New York	1-800-541-2437
North Carolina	1-800-342-2437
North Dakota	1-800-472-2180
Ohio	1-800-332-2437
Oklahoma	1-800-535-2437
Oregon	1-800-777-2437

Pennsylvania	1-800-662-6080
Puerto Rico	1-800-765-1010
Rhode Island	1-800-726-3010
South Carolina	1-800-322-2437
South Dakota	1-800-592-1861
Tennessee	1-800-525-2437
Texas	1-800-299-2437
Utah	1-800-882-2437
Virginia	1-800-533-4138
Virgin Islands	1-800-773-2437
Washington	1-800-272-2437
West Virginia	1-800-642-8244
Wisconsin	1-800-334-2437
Wyoming	1-800-327-3577

RESEARCH FOUNDATIONS

AMFAR/American Foundation for AIDS Research
733 Third Avenue, 12th Floor
New York, New York 10017-3204
Phone: 212-682-7440
AMFAR, founded by actress Elizabeth Taylor and Dr. Mathilde Krim, is a nonprofit organization dedicated to AIDS research and treatment. Particularly committed to education and prevention. A good resource for current information about HIV/AIDS.

Magic Johnson Foundation
2029 Century Park East, Suite 810
Los Angeles, California 90067
Phone: 301-785-0201
Provides funding for AIDS research, education, and prevention. Supports community organizations, particularly those that serve minorities and teenagers.

RECOMMENDED READING:

AIDS: Information Sourcebook. Phoenix: Oryz Press, 1992.

Garrett, Laurie. *The Coming Plague.* New York: Farrar, Straus and Giroux, 1995.

Giblin, James Cross. *When Plague Strikes: The Black Death, Smallpox, AIDS.* New York: HarperCollins, 1995.

Hein, Karen, Theresa Foy DieGeronimo, and the Editors of Consumer Reports Books. *AIDS: Trading Fears for Facts: A Guide for Young People.* Yonkers, NY: Consumer Reports Books, 1989.

Jennings, Chris. *Understanding and Preventing AIDS: A Book for Everyone (2nd Edition).* Cambridge, MA: Health Alert Press, 1988.

Johnson, Earvin. *What You Can Do to Avoid AIDS.* New York: Times Books, 1992.

Madaras, Lynda. *Lynda Madaras Talks to Teens About AIDS: An Essential Guide For Parents, Teachers, and Young People.* New York: Newmarket Press, 1988.

Mann, Jonathan, Thomas Netter, and Daniel Tarantola. *AIDS in the World.* Cambridge, MA: Harvard University Press, 1992.

Shilts, Randy. *And the Band Played On: Politics, People, and the AIDS Epidemic.* New York: St. Martin's Press, 1987.

Stine, Gerald J. *AIDS Update: 1994–1995.* Englewood Cliffs, NJ: Prentice-Hall, 1995.

White, Ryan, and Anne Marie Cunningham. *My Own Story.* New York: Dial Books, 1991.

FILMS AND VIDEOS

AIDS. InVision Communications, 1994.

And the Band Played On. HBO Home Video, 1993.

Growing Up in the Age of AIDS, ABC News, 1992.

Philadelphia. Columbia TriStar Home Video, 1993.

Time Out: The Truth About AIDS. Arsenio Hall Communications, Ltd., in association with Paramount Pictures, 1992.

What About Sex? Teens Speak Out About Parents, Peers, & Personal Responsibility. BMC Video, 1994.

Index